DATE DUE		
MAY 5 '88'S		
APR 1 91'S		
MAY 0 9 1994 S		
JUL 0 8 1999		
JUL 3 0 1999		

Theory of the Modern Drama

Theory and History of Literature
Edited by Wlad Godzich and Jochen Schulte-Sasse

Theory of the Modern Drama

Peter Szondi

A Critical Edition

Edited and Translated by Michael Hays

Foreword by Jochen Schulte-Sasse

Theory and History of Literature, Volume 29

University of Minnesota Press, Minneapolis

This work was supported by a grant from the Translations Program of the National Endowment for the Humanities, an independent Federal agency.

This book was originally published in Germany as *Theorie des modernen Dramas*, copyright © 1965 by Suhrkamp Verlag.

An earlier version of Part One, edited and translated by Michael Hays, appeared in *Boundary 2* 11, no. 3 (Spring 1983).

Published by the University of Minnesota Press
2037 University Avenue Southeast, Minneapolis MN 55414.
Published simultaneously in Canada
by Fitzhenry & Whiteside Limited, Markham.
Printed in the United States of America.

Library of Congress Cataloging-in-Publication Data

Szondi, Peter.
  Theory of the modern drama.

  (Theory and history of literature ; v. 29)
  Translation of: Theorie des modernen Dramas.
  Includes index.
  1. Drama—19th century—History and criticism.
2. Drama—20th century—History and criticism. I. Title.
II. Series.
PN1851.S9513 1986   809.2   86-19302
ISBN 0-8166-1284-6
ISBN 0-8166-1285-4 (pbk.)

The University of Minnesota
is an equal-opportunity
educator and employer.

Contents

Foreword
On the Difference between
a Mimetic and a Semiotic Theory
of the Modern Drama
Jochen Schulte-Sasse

I.

In the thirty years since it was originally published, Peter Szondi's *Theory of the Modern Drama* (1956) has become one of the more successful works in literary criticism, both in intellectual and in economic terms.[1] But astonishment that it has taken this long to translate the book into English must be accompanied by another question: Are there still cogent reasons why after thirty years this book should be introduced to an English-speaking audience?

Some of the minor reasons for an affirmative answer to this question are obvious: Over the last decade Szondi has been widely recognized as a seminal literary critic. His *Theory of the Modern Drama* is an early, amazingly well developed example of his critical method. Furthermore, this book—written in the most precise and polished critical discourse imaginable—contains so many suggestive and precise insights into the history of modern drama and related issues such as film aesthetics and its relation to epic features prevalent in modern drama and theater that these strengths alone might justify the belated publication of this book in English. But to my mind there is a more important reason. Szondi's *Theory of the Modern Drama* can be seen as a counterpart to Georg Lukács's *Theory of the Novel*. In 1958 Adorno hailed the latter as a book distinguished by its "depth and dashing conception" that "set a standard for philosophical aesthetics which has been maintained ever since."[2] Consequently, Lukács's essay has been widely acknowledged as a key work in the philosophy of literature, generating books several times its own length.[3] Szondi's book might therefore have been worthy of translation if he had simply repeated for the drama what Lukács had done for the novel.

But Szondi does not just duplicate Lukács's achievement for another genre; there are distinct differences between the two books in terms of their historicophilosophical foundations and their readiness to branch out into a diagnosis of the times. I will start from a comparison of the similarities and differences between the two books to lay the groundwork for a critique of Szondi's historicophilosophical and semiotic presuppositions. What Paul de Man has said in reference to Lukács's *Theory of the Novel*, namely that its "weakness and strength exist on a meaningful philosophical level,"[4] can also be said about the *Theory of the Modern Drama*. Its achievements are linked with its method, and its method is rooted in philosophical presuppositions that have to be uncovered to know how far Szondi's results might reach.

II.

Szondi acknowledges three sources for his own approach; besides Lukács's work he mentions Walter Benjamin's *Origins of the German Tragic Drama* and Adorno's *Philosophy of Modern Music*. All three publications made use of Hegel's dialectical notion of the form-content relationship, insisting that aesthetic *forms* also need interpretation and that discordant forms reflecting a tension between the thematic and formal features of an artistic work can be as significant as harmonious ones. Furthermore, all three are indebted to Hegel's diagnosis of modernity, that is, of bourgeois society, as a system of social relations dominated by the "force of division and difference." Early on Hegel had recognized that the French Revolution was an event of global historical proportions that had to be understood as the decisive attempt of bourgeois industrial society to constitute itself politically. He interpreted the objectification of all social relations in modernity not sociocritically and pessimistically as a cultural decline, as the deterioration of an originally harmonious world, but as a necessary precondition for the possibility of free subjectivity.

Hegel's refusal to glorify a state of original harmony left few traces in Lukács's *Theory of the Novel*, which starts out with a hymnic celebration of that very state:

> Happy are those ages when the starry sky is the map of all the possible paths—ages whose paths are illuminated by the light of the stars. Everything in such ages is new and yet familiar, full of adventure and yet their own. The world is wide and yet it is like a home . . . each action of the soul becomes meaningful and rounded in this duality: complete in meaning—in sense—and complete for the senses; rounded because the soul rests within itself even while it acts.[5]

The literature of this age, the epic, reflects in Lukács's view a community that "is an organic—and therefore intrinsically meaningful—concrete totality" (p. 67). He perceives the novel, in contrast, as the artistic form of an

> age in which the extensive totality of life is no longer directly given, in which the immanence of meaning in life has become a problem, yet which still thinks in terms of totality. . . . The epic gives form to a totality that is rounded; the novel seeks, by giving form, to uncover and construct the concealed totality of life. The given structure of the object (i.e. the search, which is only a way of expressing the subject's recognition that neither objective life nor its relationship to the subject is spontaneously harmonious in itself) supplies an indication of the form-giving intention. All the fissures and rents which are inherent in the historical situation must be drawn into the form-giving process and cannot nor should be disguised by compositional means. (pp. 56, 60)

Although Lukács attempts to concentrate on the historicophilosophical reasons that determined the transition from the epic to the novel—an attempt that partly counterbalances the romantic, nostalgic undertones of his essay, it is obvious that social critique is one of the driving forces of his discourse. That social critique acknowledges, to be sure, that the harmonious state of Greek culture is irretrievable and obsolete (see p. 33: "the circle whose closed nature was the transcendental essence of [Greek] life has, for us, been broken; we cannot breathe in a closed world"). Nevertheless, his analysis gains its impetus from a desire to overcome existing conditions.

Szondi obviously does not share this desire. One effect this has on his study is the lack of any in-depth interpretation of paradigmatic examples of the traditional dramatic form. He is content to reconstruct some ideal-typical features of that form. These features serve as background for what holds his real interest, namely the process of disintegration and fragmentation of established cultural formations. In comparison to the balance characteristic of Lukács's treatment of the two ages, which simultaneously is a balance between nostalgia and the historicophilosophical conviction that nostalgia is unjustified, Szondi's essay seems uneven. This unevenness, though, has its roots in the author's methodological convictions. Szondi is fascinated with moments of transition and crisis because they create tensions, discrepancies, epistemologically productive ruptures on which the critic can dwell and from which he can comprehend social features as features of difference. In other words, Szondi expands and radicalizes Lukács's observation that we could no longer breathe in a mythic, closed world epistemologically. The critic, striving to grasp the form-content dialectic and its relation to social structure, is forced to utilize moments of crisis as epistemological tools in his or her cognitive efforts.

This method explains why Szondi felt a life-long fascination for the Early

Romantics who had developed similar insights. The first article he published, at age 25, was an essay on "Friedrich Schlegel and Romantic Irony," in which he connected Schlegel's characterization of the modern novel as a form that can "hover on wings of poetic reflection between the depiction and the author of the depiction, perpetually intensify this reflection, and multiply it as in an endless series of mirrors" with Lukács's characterization of the novel:

> With this important first step toward a theory of the novel (which was subsequently elaborated by Georg Lukács), this form appears as the modern equivalent of the epic. The epic was the depiction of the entire world in a presubjectivist period whose wholeness was never questioned and which was unaware of the split between the ego and the world. In the modern age, which has been marked by this split at least since Kant, the reconciliation of the subjective with the objective in the work of art has seemed impossible.[6]

Unlike Lukács, the critic Szondi makes himself at home in the realm of consciousness represented by the novel and by Romantic irony. The absence of nostalgia is matched by the absence of a utopian perspective.

III.

I will return to the strange intersecting of voices indicated in the last paragraph (Schlegel, Hegel on Schlegel, Lukács on Hegel and Schlegel, Szondi on the last three, and, in addition, Paul de Man on all of them). At this point I would like to elaborate briefly on the background against which Szondi projects his comprehension of the form-content dialectic of the modern drama. Lukács's treatment of the epic as a form-content dialectic reflecting mythic, harmonious ages is reminiscent of the tripartite historicophilosophical scheme of German Enlightenment and Idealism. The epic corresponds to the idealization of Greek culture in, for instance, Schiller's essay *On Naive and Sentimental Literature* (1795); the category of the naive in Schiller is functionally equivalent to the category of the epic in Lukács. Lukács's historical scheme is thus not purely Hegelian; it is a combination of Schiller and Hegel, which explains its nostalgic features and its utopian dimension. Schiller's legacy in that scheme anticipates Lukács's later turn to a Marxist philosophy of history more than Hegel's legacy does.

There is no similar dependency on the eighteenth century's tripartite historicophilosophical scheme in Szondi's reconstruction of the history of the drama. For, interestingly enough, Szondi does not simply replace the form-content dialectic of the epic with that of the "absolute drama," likewise relating it to a historicophilosophical era of original harmony. Lukács, and Szondi after him, characterized the age of the epic as a totality whose wholeness was never questioned by those living at the time. The epic is, to repeat Szondi's formulation, "the depiction of an *entire* world in a *presubjectivist* period." This means that the age of the epic could not have generated a form like the absolute drama which is, as Szondi makes clear enough, the form of an age that represents itself in the aesthetic production of interpersonal relations: "The Drama of modernity came into being in the Renaissance. It was the result of a bold intellectual effort made by a newly self-conscious being who, after the collapse of the medieval worldview, sought to create an artistic reality within which he could fix and mirror himself on the basis of interpersonal relationships alone" (p. 7). In other words, the historical emergence of the absolute drama already presupposes a relative juxtaposition of subject and object in the consciousness of this age. The distance between subject and object is here, to be sure, not yet perceived as an unreconcilable split — a split reflecting the development of objective conditions that are able to determine and change the subjectivity of the subject.

Lukács had argued that the transition from the epic to the novel was caused by the intrusion of time: "Time can become constitutive only when the bond with the transcendental home has been severed. . . . In the novel, meaning is separated from life, and hence the essential from the temporal; we might almost say that the entire inner action of the novel is nothing but a struggle against the power of time" (p. 122). Contrary to what Lukács says about the drama (p. 126), time undoubtedly has entered the world of the absolute drama even if the subject is conceived of as being able to sublate the effect of time, to reconcile the differences being brought about by the inroads of time. For time does not need to be considered an independent "power of transformation" to become problematic. In other words, there is an early modern perception of time, a breach of the timeless wholeness supposedly constitutive for the age of the epic, that shapes the form-content relationship of the absolute drama. This is clearly reflected in the thematics of the plays of Schiller, who paradoxically was one of the early major thinkers to recognize the inroads made by the divisions and differences in modernity, and who at the same time can serve as a paradigmatic absolute dramatist in Szondi's scheme.

In his *Letters on Don Carlos*, Schiller wrote: "a benevolence that was subsequently to extend over the whole of humanity would have to proceed from a more intimate bond,"[7] referring to the friendship in his play between a future king, Don Carlos, and a politician, Marquis Posa. Schiller considered an increase in "intimate bonds" to be both a political precondition for any humanization of society and the most natural aim of aesthetic pleasure. In the letters accompanying his play he therefore wanted to speak "about a favorite topic of our decade — about the spread of more pure, gentle humanity, about the highest possible freedom of *individuals*, along with the highest blossoming of the state, in short about the most perfect condition of mankind" (p. 33). It becomes clear a bit later just what the object of his attention was, as well as the fact that he perceived it as a public concern and not just a private one: "I am neither an Illuminati nor a Mason, but if both fraternal orders have a moral purpose in common, and if this purpose is the most important for society, then it must be at least very closely related to the one that Marquis Posa proposed" (p. 337). In 1785 and 1786, Schiller had immersed himself in the vehement, public discussion of the Illuminati then raging, and he had read the writings of the order's founder Adam Weishaupt. The theory of the Illuminati as of so many other freemasonries was based on the premise that only the moral improvement of a state's citizenry and not the overthrow of its government would bring about positive changes in the political condition of society. Change—both in the state and in society—depended upon principles of social interaction that could be influenced positively only by individuals. For the Illuminati, as for Schiller, the key was the "intimate bonds" of friendship. The order, like most Masonic groups, conceived of itself as an oversized amalgamation of friends, whose principles, functioning in small groups, were supposed to spread gradually through society, eventually permeating all aspects of political life, including the behavior of the rulers. Schiller's reference to the dominant topic of contemporary political discussion and his parallel construction of Posa's plans is hardly accidental: in the 1780s, he too saw close personal friendships and larger, organized groups of friends as the point of crystallization for the moral renewal of society and the state.

Szondi's reconstruction of the absolute drama makes it clear that such thematic concerns, no matter how varied they might be in detail, determine the form of the absolute drama as well, and that this shift from thematics to form constituted a form-content dialectic that had as its basis the unbroken belief that social totality could be reproduced and mirrored in interpersonal relationships. Szondi's reconstructions, though, evidently do not share the historicophilosophical ambitions of Schiller, Hegel, and Lukács. Historicophilosophically, *his* reconstructions are open-ended on both sides of the chronological continuum because they do not idolize a state of original harmony, of an absolute origin. Nor does his argument imply that current divisions should or could be sublated in a future harmonious state. The question remains whether this open-endedness can escape a basic presupposition of the Hegelian form-content dialectic: The presupposition that art is a fundamentally mimetic discourse, reflecting dominant features of social totality. In my view, Szondi's epistemologically and methodologically motivated interest in ruptures ultimately turns out to be insufficiently radical; his belief in the mimetic nature of art neutralizes his critical methodology.

IV.

I have already indicated that in his *Theory of the Novel* Lukács had cited Schlegel's concept of irony affirmatively:

The self-recognition and, with it, self-abolition of subjectivity was called irony by the first theoreticians of the novel, the aesthetic philosophers of early Romanticism. As a formal constituent of the novel form this signifies an interior diversion of the normatively creative subject into subjectivity as interiority, which opposes power complexes that are alien to it and which strives to imprint the contents of its longing upon the alien world, and a subjectivity which sees through the abstract and, therefore, limited nature of the mutually alien worlds of subject and object, understand[s] these worlds by seeing their limitations as necessary conditions of their existence and, by thus seeing through them, allows the duality of the world to subsist. At the same time the creative subjectivity glimpses a unified world in the mutual relativity of elements essentially alien to one another, and gives form to this world.[8]

As Paul de Man has argued in the essay mentioned above, Lukács seems to free himself here "from preconceived notions about the novel as an imitation of reality." Irony, de Man continues, "steadily undermines this claim at imitation and substitutes for it a conscious, interpreted awareness of the distance that separates an actual experience from the understanding of this experience."[9] As I have argued in an introduction to another book in this series, [10] de Man's semiotic understanding of Romantic irony indeed comes very close to the semiotic foundation of the concept of irony in Early Romanticism. Novalis, for instance, was fascinated by the duplicity constitutive of any act of representation: "The nature of identity can be demonstrated only by a pseudo-sentence of identity [since the formula $A = A$ expresses a simultaneity of sameness and otherness]. . . . We leave the identical in order to represent it." By emphasizing the "re" in representation, that is, by stressing the duplicity of being and representation that can never be sublated or conflated, Novalis conceives of representation as something that necessarily undermines any metaphysics of presence. This makes it logically impossible to conceive of art as a mimetic discourse, at least if one applies the rather narrow definition of mimesis or imitation underlying the Hegelian notion of form-content dialectics.[11]

But Lukács never really freed himself "from preconceived notions about the novel as an imitation of reality" when he appropriated the Romantic concept of irony for his own purposes. Disregarding what Hegel had to say about Friedrich Schlegel and the Romantic concept of irony (cf., for instance: "The general meaning of . . . irony is a concentration of the ego in and on itself—an ego for which all bonds are broken and that only wants to live in the bliss of self-enjoyment. This irony was invented by Herr Friedrich von Schlegel, and many others have repeated it" and so forth),[12] Lukács interprets Romantic irony from a Hegelian point of view. He sees the force of difference and alienation, which according to Hegel entered history with the emergence of modern societies, as a historical precondition for the ironical self's free activity. In reflecting upon the limitations engendered by the forces of difference and alienation, the ironical self frees him- or herself from those limitations. Lukács obviously combines the Romantic notion of free activity with Hegel's reflection on the duality of rational domination over nature as a precondition of human freedom and the inroads of difference and alienation that domination engendered. He therefore can suppress the semiotic foundations of Romantic irony which would collapse any comprehension of art as an imitation of life and can conceive of Romantic subjectivity as an objectified manifestation of modernity, not as an activity that should be fostered despite its fundamental inability to achieve what it sets out to achieve. As an observed, juxtaposed subject, Romantic subjectivity displays for Lukács the same ruptured, discrepant form-content dialectics he sees represented in the novel. His method arrests subjectivity in an interpreted image and never reflects it as an agency of self-representations.

The question is to what extent does Szondi share Lukács's emphasis on the mimetic nature of art? When he says of Schlegel's concept of irony: "Directness of expression has given way to self-consciousness. . . . Life is contemplated from the perspective of a 'deep and infinite meaning' that is not immanent to it,"[13] Szondi seems to come close to a semiotic understanding of art that starts from the duplicity of being and its representation. The same can be said of a statement in Szondi's interpretation of Benjamin's *City Portraits*: "The tension between name and reality, which is the origin of poetry, is only experienced painfully, as the distance separating man from things."[14] But a closer look reveals that these remarks are always compatible with a Hegelian notion of the historical emergence and decline of specific form-content relationships.

Adequate forms emerge only after periods of crisis. Szondi conceives of the emergence of adequate historical forms as a semiotic struggle whose outcome is predetermined. Talking about "the process by which reality becomes an image," Szondi quotes Benjamin: "Finding words for what lies before one's eyes—how hard that can be! But when they do come they strike against reality with little hammers until they have knocked the image out of it, as out of copper plate."[15] The Hegelian implications of these remarks become clear when he adds: "The competition between the two [name and reality] always ends, to be sure, with the victory of objective reality." From here it is not far to statements that presuppose a rather narrow notion of the aesthetic reflection of reality, as when he says, in his *Theory of the Modern Drama*, that the aesthetic realm "is supposed to *reflect*", that is, to represent, "the conversion and dispersal of historical process" (p. 36). Paul de Man's critique of Szondi's interpretation of the Romantic concept of irony as a "belief in the reconciliation of the ideal and the real as the result of an action or the activity of the mind"[16] can, if read against the background of his critique of Lukács, help us understand Szondi's representational presuppositions as well. His interpretation of the history of dramatic forms is rooted in a mimetic concept of art.

V.

From here the intertwining of Szondi's method with his reconstruction of the history of the drama *and* the shortcomings of that reconstruction should become apparent. His reconstruction is unable not only to comprehend but to even notice other forms of the modern drama. There are at least two such forms; they are located on either side of the spectrum Szondi's method covers. In the direction of a radical notion of art as an imitation of reality, one that does not share the open-endedness of Szondi's historical philosophy and starts from a closed notion of history, plays can be found that attempt to preserve major features of the absolute drama while simultaneously trying to overcome an idealist notion of the subject as an independent and self-identical agent. I am referring to allegorical forms developed by Marxist playwrights such as Peter Hacks, Heiner Müller, and Helmut Lange.[17]

There is, to be sure, a decisive difference between the dramatic form these playwrights developed and the form of the absolute drama described by Szondi: The microcosm and the macrocosm in these plays are no longer united or related organically (cf. p. 36); rather their relation to one another is discrepant. An adequate understanding of them requires two readings: For the microcosm of the play, a literal reading of human interaction and, for the macrocosm, an allegorical reading of the historical development of human society. Such forms, of course, presuppose a self-assured epistemology that is completely alien to Szondi's epistemological skepticism and to the dependence of his critical method on the breakthrough of historical and formal difference in moments of crisis.

More importantly, neither Szondi's reconstruction of the history of drama nor his Hegelian notion of the form-content relationship leave space for a dramatic form based on a semiotic understanding of theatrical practice. Although numerous examples of such practice exist, for example, Piscator's theater productions in Weimar Germany, Brecht's epic theater, forms of living theater from the 1920s to the early 1970s, contemporary feminist theater productions like those of At the Foot of the Mountain and the Women's Theater Project, two feminist theaters in Minneapolis, I will use Brecht's *Lehrstücktheorie* (insufficiently translatable as "theory of didactic plays") as an illustration of twentieth-century tendencies to develop a critical semiotic understanding of theatrical practice. In its theoretical aspects, if not in its practical realizations, Brecht's conception of such a theatrical practice is by far the most advanced form.

Brecht had always conceived of the epic theater, for which he gained fame, as a transitional form of theatrical practice that still accepts and performs within the restricted framework of the institution of bourgeois theater. He called the social intentions of his epic theater the "little pedagogy," contrasting it to a theater of the future, the concept of which he developed under the name of "great pedagogy".

The Great Pedagogy alters the role of acting completely. . . . It eliminates the system [i.e., the division] of actor and viewer . . . it only knows actors who simultaneously are students, according to the principle "where the interest of the individual coincides with the interest of the state, the comprehended gesture determines the mode of operation of the individual." [Here] imitating acting becomes the major part of pedagogy. . . . In contrast, the Little Pedagogy achieves only a democratization of the theater during the transitional period of the first revolution. [In the theater of the Little Pedagogy] the duality [of stage and house] remains intact.[18]

Underlying the intention of eliminating the duality of house and stage is Brecht's conviction that, first, any successful and momentous learning process has to be grounded in concrete, bodily experience of attitudes or social action and that, second, only the successive experience of adverse, mutually exclusive attitudes or actions in modes of "imitating acting" will have a lasting effect. Thus, he wants actors to play different, conflicting roles during the same performance for them to learn, that is, to experience, the effect of a specific social behavior bodily. In other words, actors, now acting for themselves, should experience the ideological difference of binary attitudes on their own bodies through constant role changes.

In a way, Brecht sees the same epistemological dependency of human cognition on spaces of difference as Szondi does, except that he grounds this conviction materialistically and insists that a theatrical practice that produces such spaces can be created. Furthermore, he does not orient such a practice toward cognitive results that arrest the learning process. Because of the problematic nature of self-representation, of the duplicity of representation and being, Brecht conceived of the "great pedagogy" as a medium that opens up an endless road of self-representations on which we can always only approximate an understanding of our being. Such representations are not geared toward contemplative cognition but rather toward social praxis.

Such modes of theatrical practice, based on the unsublatable duality of experience and representation, had to fall through the net of Szondi's Hegelian categories. Nevertheless, if one does not read Szondi's depiction of modern drama as an inclusive one, this book offers an understanding of the epic tendencies in the modern theater that is rich in insight and in many ways still unparalleled.

Translator's Preface

In the introductory section of this book, Peter Szondi indicates that one of the primary assumptions underlying his critical practice is that the form of a work "provides evidence about human existence." Having made this bold assertion, he can go on to say that the dramatic forms he intends to investigate should, therefore, be identified as literary-historical phenomena, as "documents" of human history. Anyone who has read his other critical work knows that Szondi applies this principle not only to dramatic texts but to textual production in general. A fundamental aspect of Szondi's hermeneutic method is constituted by his search for the moment of tension between form and content that will reveal the historical ground on which a text is built. It is also this desire to allow the text to "speak," to announce its own historicity, that emerges in his decision not to add to or substantially revise this book when it appeared in a new edition some ten years after its original composition (see his afterword to the 1963 edition in this volume).

As editor and translator of this edition, I have chosen to honor this important critical principle in the hope that the reader will not only discover a new way of approaching the development of the modern drama, but that she or he will also note the historical boundaries of Szondi's own rhetoric. Thus it is that I have kept certain rhetorical turns and critical formulations that, given Szondi's often very advanced theoretical insights, might well have been rendered in a style more in keeping with current poststructuralist discourse. This is also the reason I have let stand the masculine pronoun where today one might prefer to find a less gender-bound formulation. One should not, however, in the name of a more

democratic usage, be prevented from noting the historical valences of such supposedly neutral terms as *Mensch*—and their essentially masculine orientation
when employed by Szondi and his contemporaries.

There are, of course, certain difficulties that must remain unresolved: word
play and turns of phrase that simply do not have an English equivalent. I have
tried to retain the core of these locutions in the translation, but in so doing the
range as well as the playfulness of Szondi's language has sometimes suffered ir-
reparable damage. To restore something of what has been lost, I have appended
a series of notes and comments that I hope will help guide the reader through
some of these difficult spots and to a better understanding of the sources and the
implications of Szondi's language and critical orientation. I hope, too, that this
translation can serve as a token of the esteem in which Peter Szondi was held
by all those who studied under him in Berlin and elsewhere.

M. H.

Part One

Introduction
Historical Aesthetics
and Genre-Based Poetics

Theorists of the drama have condemned the presence of epic features in dramatic works ever since Aristotle. But anyone who attempts to describe the development of recent drama can (for reasons he ought to clarify for himself and his readers) no longer feel called upon to make such judgments.*

In earlier dramatic theory, the expectation that one adhere to formal rules was justified by a particular notion of form, one that recognized neither a historical nor a dialectical relationship between form and content. The assumption was that a preexisting form was embodied in dramatic art through its union with a subject matter chosen with this form in mind. If the preexistent form was not adequately realized—if the drama possessed any forbidden epic features—the error was attributed to the selection of subject matter. In the *Poetics*, Aristotle insists that the poet must remember not to "write a tragedy on an *epic* body of incident (i.e., one with a plurality of stories in it), by attempting to dramatize, for instance, the entire *Iliad*."[1] Even Goethe and Schiller's effort to distinguish between epic and dramatic poetry had as its practical goal the avoidance of faulty subject matter.[2]

This traditional view, which is based on an initial separation of form and content, admits of no historical classification either. The preexistent form is historically indifferent, only subject matter is historically bound. By conforming to this pattern, which is common to all prehistorical theories,* the drama appears to be the historical embodiment of atemporal form.

*Asterisks correspond to explanatory information in the Editor's Notes and Commentary.

3

That dramatic form is conceived of as existing outside history also means that such drama can always be written and can be called for in the poetics of any age.

This connection between a transhistorical poetics and an undialectical conception of form and content is restated in that culminating moment of dialectical and historical thought—the works of Hegel.* In his *Science of Logic*, he states that "the only true works of art are those whose content and form prove to be completely identical."[3] This identity is dialectical in nature: earlier in the same discussion Hegel asserts the "absolute correlation of content and form, . . . their reversion into one another, so that content is nothing but the reversion of form into content and form nothing but the reversion of content into form."[4] Identifying form and content in this way destroys the opposition between the timeless and the historical found in the old conceptual relationship. The result is the historicization of the concept "form" and, ultimately, of genre poetics (*Gattungspoetik*) itself. The lyric, epos, and drama are transformed from systematic into historical categories.

After this change in the fundamental principles of poetics, three paths remained open to critics. They could conclude that traditional poetics' three primary categories had lost their *raison d'être* along with their systematic character—thus Benedetto Croce exiled them from aesthetics.* In diametrical opposition to this view stand the efforts made to flee from a historically based poetics, from concrete literary modes, back to the timeless. E[mil] Staiger's *Poetik* (along with R. Hartl's rather unrewarding *Versuch einer psychologischen Grundlegung der Dichtungsgattungen*) bears witness to this effort. In Staiger's work, the genres are anchored in mankind's various modes of being and, finally, in the three "ecstasies" of time. That this redefinition alters the nature of poetics in general and particularly the relationship of poetics to literature is evident in the unavoidable replacement of the three basic concepts, "lyric," "epos," and "drama," by "lyrical," "epic," and "dramatic."

A third possibility existed, however—to remain within the historical perspective. This led, among Hegel's followers, to works that elaborated more than a historical aesthetics for literature: G[eorg] Lukács's *Theory of the Novel*; W[alter] Benjamin's *Origins of German Tragic Drama*; Th[eodor] W. Adorno's *Philosophy of Modern Music*. Hegel's dialectical notion of the form-content relationship was turned to productive use here. Form could be conceived of as "precipitated" content.[5] The metaphor points both to the solid and lasting nature of form and to its origin in content—thus its capacity to state something.* A valid semantics of form can be developed along these lines, one in which the form-content dialectic can be viewed as a dialectic between the statements made by form and content. The possibility arises, thereby, that the statement made by the content may contradict that of the form. If, when there is an equivalence between form and content, the thematic [the subject of the content]* operates within the framework of the formal statement as a problem contained, so to speak, within something unproblematic, a contradiction arises, because the in-disputable fixed statement of the form is called into question by the content. It is this inner antinomy that causes a given literary form to become historically problematic. This book is an attempt to explain the different forms of recent works for the stage as efforts to resolve such contradictions.

This is also the reason the discussion remains within the realm of aesthetics rather than branching out into a diagnosis of the period.* The contradictions be-tween dramatic form and the problems of contemporary life should not be set down *in abstracto*. Instead, they should be examined as technical contradictions, as "difficulties," internal to the concrete work itself. Of course, it seems natural to want to define that displacement in modern theatrical works which arises from the growing problem of dramatic form in terms of a system of genres. But we will have to do without a systematic, that is, a normative, poetics—not out of any desire to avoid the inevitably negative evaluation of the epic tendencies in these plays but because a historical-dialectical view of form and content elimi-nates the possibility of a systematic poetics as such.

The terminological starting point for this analysis is simply the concept "drama." As a time-bound concept, it stands for a specific literary-historical event—namely, the drama as it arose in Elizabethan England and, above all, as it came into being in seventeenth-century France and was perpetuated in the Ger-man classical period. Since the concept provides evidence of the assertions about human existence that were precipitated in dramatic form, it identifies this form as a literary-historical phenomenon, as a "document" of human history. It serves to expose the technical demands of the drama as reflections of existential de-mands. The totality it outlines is not of a systematic but of a historico-philo-sophic nature. Since history has been ostracized to the gaps between literary forms, only by reflecting on history can these gaps be bridged.

The notion "drama" is historically bound in its origins as well as in its content. But because the form of a work of art always seems to express something un-questionable, we usually arrive at a clear understanding of such formal state-ments only at a time when the unquestionable has been questioned and the self-evident has become problematic.* It is in this light that the drama will be dealt with here—in terms of what impedes it today—and this notion of the drama will be examined as a moment of inquiry into the possibility of modern drama.

Therefore, only a particular dramaturgic form will be designated "Drama" in the following pages. Neither the clerical plays of the Middle Ages nor Shakespeare's histories belong in this category. Working within a historical frame of reference also eliminates Greek tragedy from consideration, since its being can be examined only under a different set of conditions. The adjective "dramatic," as used hereafter, will have no qualitative meaning (as it does, for example, in E[mil] Staiger's *Grundbegriffe der Poetik*).[6] It will simply express the idea "belonging to the Drama" (a "dramatic dialogue"=dialogue in the

Drama). "Theatrical works," in contrast to Drama, will be used in the largest sense to designate anything written for the stage.* If "drama" is at any time used in this sense, it will be placed within quotation marks.

Since modern theatrical works develop out of and away from the Drama itself, this development must be considered with the help of a contrasting concept. "Epic" will serve here. It designates a common structural characteristic of the epos, the story, the novel, and other genres—namely, the presence of that which has been referred to as the "subject of the epic form"[7] or the "epic *I*."[8]

Preceding the eighteen essays in which an attempt is made to apprehend this development as it manifests itself in specific texts is a discussion of the Drama itself. All that follows will refer to this analysis.

I. The Drama

The Drama of modernity came into being in the Renaissance. It was the result of a bold intellectual effort made by a newly self-conscious being who, after the collapse of the medieval worldview, sought to create an artistic reality within which he could fix and mirror himself on the basis of interpersonal relationships alone.[1] Man entered the drama only as a fellow human being, so to speak. The sphere of the "between" seemed to be the essential part of his being; freedom and obligation, will and decision the most important of his attributes. The "place" at which he achieved dramatic realization was in an act of decision and self-disclosure.* By deciding to disclose himself to his contemporary world, man transformed his internal being into a palpable and dramatic presence.* The surrounding world, on the other hand, was drawn into a rapport with him because of his disclosure and thereby first achieved dramatic realization. Everything prior to or after this act was, had to remain, foreign to the drama — the inexpressible as well as the expressed, what was hidden in the soul as well as the idea already alienated from its subject. Most radical of all was the exclusion of that which could not express itself — the world of objects — unless it entered the realm of interpersonal relationships.

All dramatic themes were formulated in this sphere of the "between" — for example, the struggle of passion and devoir in the Cid's position between his father and his beloved; the comic paradoxes in "crooked" interpersonal situations, such as that of Justice Adam; the tragedy of individuation as it appeared to Hebbel; the tragic conflict between Duke Ernst, Albrecht, and Agnes Bernauer.*

The verbal medium for this world of the interpersonal was the dialogue. In

7

the Renaissance, after the exclusion of prologue, chorus, and epilogue, dialogue became, perhaps for the first time in the history of the theater (excluding the monologue, which remained occasional and therefore did not constitute the form of the Drama), the sole constitutive element in the dramatic web. In this respect, the neoclassical Drama distinguishes itself not only from antique tragedy but also from medieval clerical plays, from the baroque world theater, and from Shakespeare's histories. The absolute dominance of dialogue — that is, of interpersonal communication, reflects the fact that the Drama consists only of the reproduction of interpersonal relations, is only cognizant of what shines forth within this sphere.

All this shows that the Drama is a self-contained dialectic but one that is free and redefined from moment to moment. With this in mind, the Drama's major characteristics can now be understood and described.

The Drama is absolute.* To be purely relational — that is, to be dramatic, it must break loose from everything external. It can be conscious of nothing outside itself.

The dramatist is absent from the Drama. He does not speak; he institutes discussion. The Drama is not written, it is set. All the lines spoken in the Drama are dis-closures. They are spoken in context and remain there. They should in no way be perceived as coming from the author. The Drama belongs to the author only as a whole, and this connection is just an incidental aspect of its reality as a work.

The same absolute quality exists with regard to the spectator. The lines in a play are as little an address to the spectator as they are a declaration by the author. The theatergoer is an observer — silent, with hands tied, lamed by the impact of this other world. This total passivity will, however (and therein lies the dramatic experience), be converted into irrational activity. He who was the spectator is pulled into the dramatic event, becomes the person speaking (through the mouths of all the characters, of course). The spectator-Drama relationship is one of complete separation or complete identity, not one in which the spectator invades the Drama or is addressed through the Drama.

The stage shaped by the Renaissance and the neoclassical period, the much-maligned "picture-frame" stage, is the only one adequate to the absoluteness of the drama and bears witness to it in each of its features. It is no more connected to the house (by steps, for example) than the Drama is connected (stepwise) to the audience. The stage becomes visible, thus exists, only at the beginning of the play — often, in fact, only after the first lines have been spoken. Because of this, it seems to be created by the play itself. At the end of the act, when the curtain falls, the stage is again withdrawn from the spectator's view, taken back as if it were part of the play. The footlights which illuminate it create the impression that the play sheds its own light on stage.

Even the actor's art is subservient to the absoluteness of the Drama. The actor-role relationship should not be visible. Indeed, the actor and the character should unite to create a single personage.

That the Drama is absolute can be expressed in a different manner: the Drama is primary. It is not a (secondary) representation of something else (primary); it presents itself, is itself. Its action, like each of its lines, is "original"; it is accomplished as it occurs. The Drama has no more room for quotation than it does for variation. Such quotation would imply that the Drama referred to whatever was quoted. Variation would call into question the Drama's quality of being primary ("true") and present it as secondary (as a variation of something and as one variation among many). Furthermore, it would be necessary to assume a "quoter" or "varier" on whom the Drama would depend.

The Drama is primary. This also explains why historical plays always strike one as "undramatic." The attempt to stage *Luther the Reformer* requires some reference to history. If it were possible, in the absolute dramatic situation, to show Luther in the process of deciding to reform the faith, the Reformation Drama could be said to exist. But at this point, a second problem arises: the objective conditions which are necessary to motivate the decision demand epic treatment. An interpersonal portrayal of Luther's situation would be the only possible foundation for the Drama, but this account would be understandably alien to the intent of a Reformation play.

Because the Drama is always primary, its internal time is always the present. That in no way means that the Drama is static, only that time passes in a particular manner: the present passes and becomes the past and, as such, can no longer be present on stage. As the present passes away, it produces change, a new present springs from its antithesis. In the Drama, time unfolds as an absolute, linear sequence in the present. Because the Drama is absolute, it is itself responsible for this temporal sequence. It generates its own time. Therefore, every moment must contain the seeds of the future. It must be "pregnant with futurity."[2] This is possible because of the Drama's dialectical structure, which, in turn, is rooted in interpersonal relationships.

From this point of view, the demand that one adhere to the unity of time acquires new meaning. Temporal fragmentation of the scenes in a play would subvert the principle of absolute presence and linearity because every scene would have its own antecedents and results (past and future) external to the play. The individual scenes would thus be relativized. In addition, only when each scene in succession generates the next (the kind of progression necessary to the Drama) can the implicit presence of a *monteur* be avoided. The (spoken or unspoken) "three years later" presupposes an epic *I*.

A comparable set of conditions leads to the demand for unity of place. As with time, the spectator should not be conscious of a larger spatial context. Only then can an absolute—that is, a dramatic—scene arise. The more frequent the change in scene, the more difficult this is to accomplish. Besides, spatial fragmentation (like temporal) assumes an epic *I*. (Cliché: Now we will leave the conspirators in the forest and return to the unsuspecting king in his palace.)

It is generally agreed that Shakespeare's plays differ most markedly from the French neoclassical form in these two areas. But his loose and multiplace succession of scenes should be examined in conjunction with the histories (e.g., *Henry V*) in which a narrator, designated "Chorus," presents the individual acts to the audience as chapters in a popular history.

The insistence on motivation and the exclusion of accident are also based in the absoluteness of the Drama. The accidental enters the Drama from outside, but, by motivating it, accident is domesticated; it is rooted in the heart of drama itself.

Ultimately, the whole world of the Drama is dialectical in origin. It does not come into being because of an epic *I* which permeates the work. It exists because of the always achieved and, from that point, once again disrupted sublation of the interpersonal dialectic, which manifests itself as speech in the dialogue. In this respect as well, the dialogue carries the Drama. The Drama is possible only when dialogue is possible.

II. The Drama in Crisis

The first five essays focus on Ibsen (1828–1906), Chekhov (1860–1904), Strindberg (1849–1912), Maeterlinck (1862–1949), and Hauptmann (1862–1946) because the search for the initial situation in which the modern play arose must begin with a confrontation between works from the late nineteenth century and the phenomena of the classic Drama just described.

Of course, it could well be asked whether this kind of back reference might not subvert the historical purpose of the analysis and lead one to fall back into the kind of systematic normative poetics rejected in the introduction—especially since that which was tentatively described in the preceding pages as the Drama arising in the Renaissance coincides with the traditional conception of the Drama. It is identical with that which handbooks on dramatic technique (e.g., Gustav Freytag's) taught and against which modern plays were at first and, occasionally, still are measured by critics. But the historical method, applied here to glean information from the form about the historicity of this "normative" Drama, is in no danger of becoming normative itself— even if theatrical works from the turn of the century are examined in terms of the Drama's historical image. After all, around 1860 this form for the Drama not only was the subjective norm of the theorists but also represented the objective state of the works of the period. Whatever else there was at hand that might have been played off against this form was either archaic in character or tied to a specific thematic. The "open" Shakespearean form, for example, which is constantly compared with the "closed" neoclassical form, cannot really be detached from Shakespeare's histories. Whenever it was successfully employed in German literature, it served the purpose of historical fresco (*Götz von Berlichingen, Danton's Death*).

The connection established in what follows is, therefore, not normative in origin; rather, it will deal conceptually with objective-historical relationships. To be sure, the relationship to neoclassical dramatic form is different for each of the five dramatists discussed here. Ibsen did not take a critical stance vis-à-vis traditional dramatic form. He achieved fame in great part because of his mastery of earlier dramatic conventions. But this external perfection masked an internal crisis in the Drama. Chekhov also adopted the traditional form. He no longer had any firm commitment to the *pièce bien faite* (into which the neoclassical Drama had alienated itself) though. On this inherited terrain he constructed a magical, poetic edifice that nonetheless has no autonomous style, gives no guarantee of a formal whole, and, instead, continually exposes the bases of its construction. Thus, he revealed the discrepancy between the form he used and that demanded by his thematic. And if Strindberg and Maeterlinck came upon new forms, they did so only after a conflict with the tradition. Then again, sometimes this conflict remained unresolved and visible within their works—a signpost, as it were, on the road to the forms developed by later dramatists. Finally, Hauptmann's *Before Sunrise* and *The Weavers* allow us to see the problems created for the drama by a social thematic.

1. Ibsen

Access to the problems of form in a play like *Rosmersholm* has been hampered by the idea of an analytical technique, which has led Ibsen's work to be compared with that of Sophocles.* If, however, one is aware of the aesthetic connections in relation to which Sophocles' analysis was employed and how it was discussed in the correspondence between Goethe and Schiller,* the notion ceases to be an obstacle and, in fact, turns out to be the key to Ibsen's late work.

On October 2, 1797, Schiller wrote to Goethe that

> For the past few days I have been very busy trying to find a tragic subject which would be of the same sort as *Oedipus Rex*, one which would provide the poet with all the same advantages. These advantages are infinite, even if I name only one: the most compound of actions, though it militates against the tragic form, can nonetheless be its basis if the action has already taken place and so falls entirely outside the tragedy. In addition, that which has happened, because it is inalterable, is by its very nature much more terrible. The fact that something *might have* happened affects the spirit quite differently than the fear that something might happen—Oedipus is, as it were, merely a tragic analysis. Everything is already present. It is simply unfolded. That can be done with the simplest of actions and in a very short time, no mat-

ter how complicated the events were or what conditions they depended on. What an advantage for the poet! —But I am afraid that Oedipus represents a genre all its own and there is no other like species.

Half a year earlier (on April 22, 1797), Goethe had written Schiller that the exposition was hard work for a dramatist "because one expects him to produce an eternal forward movement, and I would call that dramatic material best in which the exposition is already part of the development." Schiller responded, on April 25, that *Oedipus Rex* approached this ideal to an amazing degree.

The starting point for this thought process is that the form of the drama exists a priori. The analytical technique is pressed into service to permit inclusion of the exposition in the dramatic movement and thus remove its epic effect or to permit use of the "most compound" of actions, those that at first do not seem to fit the dramatic form, as subject matter for a drama.

This is not what happens in Sophocles' *Oedipus*, however. Aeschylus' earlier, lost trilogy had already provided a chronological account of the Theban king's fate. Sophocles could forgo this epic presentation of widely separated events because it was, for him, less a question of the events themselves than of the tragic qualities they embody. This tragedy is not tied to details though; it rises above the temporal flow. The tragic dialectic of sight and loss of sight—that a man loses his sight through self-knowledge, through that one eye "too many" that he has[1]—this peripeteia (both in the Aristotelian *and* Hegelian sense) requires only a *single* act of recognition, the anagnorisis,[2] to become a dramatic reality. The Athenian spectator knew the myth; it did not have to be acted out. The only person who has yet to experience it is Oedipus himself—and *he* can do so only at the end, after the myth has become his life. Exposition is unnecessary here, and the analysis is synonymous with the action. Oedipus, blind though seeing, creates, so to speak, the empty center of a world that already knows his fate. Step by step, messengers who come from this world invade his inner being and fill it with their horrible truth. It is not a truth that belongs to the past, however. The present, not the past, is revealed. Oedipus *is* his father's murderer, his mother's husband, his children's brother. He *is* "the land's pollution"[3] and has only to learn what has been in order to recognize what is. Thus, the action in *Oedipus Rex*, although it in fact precedes the tragedy, is nonetheless contained within its present. The analytical technique is, in Sophocles' case, called for by the subject matter itself, not to reproduce a preexisting form but rather to show its tragic quality in its greatest purity and depth.

In differentiating the dramatic structures created by Ibsen and Sophocles, one is led straight to the formal problem that confronted Ibsen, a problem which exposes the historical crisis in the Drama itself. There is no need to prove that for Ibsen the analytical technique, rather than being an isolated phenomenon, is *the* mode of construction in his modern plays. It should be sufficient to remind the reader of the more important of them: *A Doll's House, Pillars of Society, Ghosts, The Lady from the Sea, Rosmersholm, The Wild Duck, The Masterbuilder, John Gabriel Borkman, When We Dead Awaken.*

The action of *John Gabriel Borkman* (1896) "passes one winter evening, at the manor house of the Rentheim family, in the neighborhood of the capital." For eight years John Gabriel Borkman, "formerly managing director of a bank," has lived in almost complete isolation in the "great gallery" of the house. The drawing room below is occupied by his wife, Gunhild. They live in the same house without ever seeing one another. Ella Rentheim, Gunhild's sister and owner of the house, lives elsewhere. Once a year she comes to see the estate manager. During these visits she speaks neither to Gunhild nor to Borkman.

The winter evening on which the play opens reunites these three people, who are chained together by the past but are at the same time profoundly estranged from one another. In the first act, Ella and Gunhild meet. "Well, Gunhild, it is nearly eight years now since we saw each other last."[4] The second act brings a discussion between Ella and Borkman. "It seems an endless time since we two met, Borkman, face to face."[5] And in the third act, John Gabriel and his wife stand opposite each other. "The last time we stood face to face — it was in the Court, when I was summoned to give an account —."[6]

Ella, who suffers from a terminal illness, wants the Borkmans' son, who was her foster child for many years, to come and stay with her again so that she will not be alone when she dies. This wish motivates the conversations in which the past of all three characters is brought into the open.

Borkman loved Ella Rentheim but married her sister, Gunhild. He spent eight years in prison for theft of bank deposits after his friend Hinkel, a lawyer, exposed him. Ella, whose fortune was the only one in the bank that Borkman left untouched, bought back the family estate for him and his wife when it was auctioned off. After he was freed, Borkman withdrew to the house and the gallery. During this period Ella raised the Borkmans' son, who was almost an adult when he returned to his mother.

These are the events. But they are not recounted here for their own sake. What lies "behind" and "between" them is essential: motives and time.

"But when you, of your own accord, undertook to educate Erhart for me — what was your motive in that?" Mrs. Borkman asks her sister.[7]

"I have often wondered what was your real reason for sparing all my property? That and that alone?" Ella asks her brother-in-law.[8]

And thus the true relationships between Ella and Borkman, Borkman and Gunhild, and Ella and Erhart are revealed.

Borkman gave up Ella in order to get Hinkel, who was also Ella's suitor, to back his career at the bank. Although he did not love Gunhild, he married her instead of Ella. But Hinkel, who was rejected by a despairing Ella, thought Borkman's influence was the cause and took vengeance by turning him in. Ella, whose life was ruined by Borkman's unfaithfulness, now loves only one person—Erhart, Borkman's son. She had raised him to be her own child, but when Erhart grew older his mother took him back. Ella, whose terminal illness was caused by that "spiritual shock," Borkman's faithlessness, now wants Erhart back during the final months of her life. But Erhart leaves both his mother and his aunt to be with the woman he loves.

Such are the motives. On this winter evening they are dragged out of the ruined souls of these three people and exposed to the glare of the footlights. But the essential has not yet been mentioned. When Borkman, Gunhild, and Ella speak of the past, it is not individual events that stand in the foreground or their motivation but time itself which is painted by them: "I shall redeem myself . . . redeem my ruined life," says Mrs. Borkman.[9] When Ella tells her she has heard that Gunhild and her husband live in the same house without seeing each other, she replies: "Yes; that is how it has been, Ella, ever since they let him out, and sent him home to me. All these long eight years."[10] And when Ella and Borkman meet:

Ella: It seems an endless time since we two met, Borkman, face to face.
Borkman (*gloomily*): It's a long, long time. And terrible things have passed since then.
Ella: A whole lifetime has passed—a wasted lifetime.[11]

A bit later:

Ella: From the day your image began to dwindle in my mind, I have lived my life as though under an eclipse. During all these years it has grown harder and harder for me—and at last utterly impossible—to love any living creature.[12]

And in the third act, when Gunhild tells her husband she has thought more than enough about his dubious past, he responds:

I too. During those five endless years in my cell—and elsewhere—I had time to think it over. And during the eight years up there in the gallery I had still more ample time. I have retried the whole case—by myself. Time after time I have retried it . . . I have paced up and down the gallery there, turning every one of my actions upside down and inside out.[13] I have skulked up there and wasted eight precious years of my life![14]

In the last act, in the open space in front of the house:

It is high time I should come out into the open air again. . . . Nearly three years in detention—five years in prison—eight years in the gallery up there—.[15]

But he has no time to get used to the fresh air. His flight out of the prison of his past does not bring him back to life. It leads to his death. And Ella and Gunhild, who on this evening lose both the man and the son they love, take each other's hands, "two shadows—over the dead man."

Here the past is not, as in Sophocles' *Oedipus*, a function of the present. On the contrary, the present is rather an occasion for conjuring up the past. The accent lies neither on Ella's fate nor on Borkman's death. No single event from the past is the thematic of the play either—not Borkman's rejection of Ella, not Hinkel's vengeance, nothing from the past. Instead, the past itself, the repeatedly mentioned "long years" and the "wasted lifetime," is the subject of the play—a subject that does not lend itself to the dramatic present. Only something temporal can be made present in the sense of dramatic actualization, not time itself. Time can only be reported about in the Drama; its direct presentation is possible solely in an art form that includes it "among its constitutive principles." This art form—as G[eorg] Lukács has shown—is the novel.[16]

"In the drama (and the epos) the past either does not exist or is completely present. Because these forms know nothing of the passage of time, they allow of no qualitative difference between the experiencing of past and present; time has no power of transformation, it neither intensifies nor diminishes the meaning of anything."[17] In *Oedipus* the analysis transforms the past into the present. "This is the formal meaning of the typical scenes of revelation and recognition which Aristotle shows us; something that was pragmatically unknown to the heroes of the drama enters their field of vision, and in the world thus altered they have to act otherwise than they might wish to act. But the force of the newly introduced factor is not diminished by a temporal perspective, it is absolutely homogeneous with and equivalent to the present."[18] Thus another difference becomes clear. Truth in *Oedipus Rex* is objective in nature. It belongs to the world. Only Oedipus lives in ignorance, and his road to the truth forms the tragic action. For Ibsen, on the other hand, truth is that of interiority. There lie the motives for the decisions that emerge in the light of day; there the traumatic effects of these decisions lie hidden and live on despite all external changes. In addition to the temporal present, Ibsen's thematic does without presence in this topical sense as well—a presence which the Drama requires. The thematic does arise out of interpersonal relationships, but it is at home only in the innermost being of these estranged and solitary figures, as a reflex of the interpersonal.

That means it is impossible to give it direct dramatic presentation. This material has need of the analytical technique, and not simply to achieve greater density. As the subject matter of a novel, which is basically what it is, it can only be staged thanks to this technique. Even so, the thematic ultimately remains alien to the stage. However much the thematic is tied to the presence (in both senses of the word) of an action, it remains exiled in the past and the depths of the individual. This is the unresolved formal problem in Ibsen's dramaturgy.[19]

Because his starting point was epic in nature, he was forced to develop an incomparable mastery of dramatic construction. Because he achieved this mastery, the epic origin of his plays was no longer visible. The dramatist's dual enterprise—to give his material presence and function—was an inexorable necessity for Ibsen. But he never quite succeeded.

A great deal of that which serves to create presence is rather surprising when examined on its own—the leitmotiv technique, for instance. It is not used, as is the case elsewhere, to indicate sameness in change or to make cross-connections. Instead, the past lives on in Ibsen's leitmotivs, conjured up by their mention. In *Rosmersholm*, for example, Beate Rosmer's suicide becomes an eternal presence because of the millpond. Symbolic events are used to link the past to the present: the tinkle of glass in an adjoining room (*Ghosts*). The motif of genetic inheritance serves more to make the past present than it does to embody the antique notion of fate: Captain Alving's conduct reappears as his son's illness. Only by way of this kind of analytical analysis is it possible, if not to present time itself—Mrs. Alving's life at the side of this person—at least to represent it as an awareness of time elapsed, as a difference in generations.

And making the material dramatically functional, which would otherwise serve to work out the causal-final structure of a unified action, here serves to bridge the gap between the present and the past—a past that cannot be presented objectively. Ibsen seldom managed to give equal status to the action in the present and the thematic action the play conjures up. They are often only rough-joined. In this respect, *Rosmersholm* again seems to be Ibsen's masterpiece. The topical political theme can hardly be separated from the internal theme of the past. This past is not hidden in the depths of the characters' souls but lives on in the house itself. Furthermore, the former makes it possible for the latter to maintain a twilight presence appropriate to its nature. They are completely united in the figure of Rector Kroll. He is both Rosmer's political enemy and brother of a woman driven to suicide—Mrs. Rosmer. But here too Ibsen fails to motivate the end of the play sufficiently in terms of the past. He fails to demonstrate its inevitability. The tragedy of a blind Oedipus led back into the palace is not accorded to Rosmer and Rebecca West when, summoned by the dead Mrs. Rosmer, they plunge into the millpond.

Here one also sees the distance from tragic fall that the bourgeois world in general enjoys. The immanent tragic condition of this world does not originate in death but in life itself.[20] This life, Rilke said (in direct reference to Ibsen), "had slipped into us, had withdrawn inward, so deeply that it was scarcely possible to conjecture about it anymore."[21] Balzac's comment belongs here too. "We all die unknown."[22]* Ibsen's work stands wholly under this sign. But because he tried to reveal this hidden life dramatically, to enact it through the dramatis personae themselves, he destroyed it. Ibsen's figures could survive only by burrowing into themselves and living off the "life lie."* Because he did not enclose them in a novel, because he did not leave them within their life but instead forced them to publicly declare themselves, he killed them. So it is that in periods which are hostile to the Drama, the dramatist becomes the murderer of the creatures he has created.

2. Chekhov

In Chekhov's plays, the characters live under the sign of renunciation — renunciation of the present and of communication before all else, renunciation of the happiness arising from real interaction. This resignation, in which passionate longing and irony mix to prevent any extreme, also determines the form of Chekhov's plays and his position in the development of modern theater.

To renounce the present is to live with memories and utopian dreams; to do without human interaction is to be lonely.* *The Three Sisters*, perhaps the most fully realized of Chekhov's plays, is exclusively a presentation of lonely individuals intoxicated by memories and dreaming of the future. Their present, overwhelmed by the past and future, is merely an interim, a period of suspended animation during which the only goal is to return to the lost homeland. This theme (around which, moreover, all romantic literature circles) becomes concrete in *The Three Sisters* in terms of the bourgeois world at the turn of the century. Thus, Olga, Masha, and Irina, the Prosorov sisters, live with their brother, Andrei Sergeovitch, in a large garrison town in East Russia. Eleven years earlier they had left their home in Moscow to go there with their father, who had taken command of a brigade. The play begins a year after their father's death. Their stay in the provinces has lost all meaning; memories of life in Moscow overflow into the boredom of their daily existence and grow into a single despairing cry: "To Moscow!"[1] The wait for this return to the past, which is also supposed to be a wonderful future, absorbs the three sisters completely. They are surrounded by garrison officers who are consumed by the same fatigue and longing. For one of these officers, though, that moment in the future which is the intended goal of the Prosorov sisters has expanded into a utopian vision. Alexander Ignatyavitch Vershinin says:

> And then, in another two or three hundred years, life on earth will be beautiful and wonderful beyond anything we can imagine. Man needs such a life and while we don't have it yet, we must become aware of its impending arrival, wait for it, imagine it, and prepare the way for it.[2]

And later,

> It seems to me that everything on earth is bound to change, little by little, and in fact it's already changing right before our eyes. Two or

three hundred years or a thousand years from now—it's immaterial how long—a new happy life will come about. Of course, we'll have no part in that life, but nevertheless even today, we live for it, work for it, well yes, suffer for it, and thus we are bringing it about. And that alone is the purpose of our existence and, if you like, in it lies our happiness.[3]

We're not meant to be happy . . . we won't be happy. . . . We must just work and work and work and someday our descendants will be happy. If I can't be happy, at least my grandchildren's grand-children. . . .[4]

Even more than this utopian orientation, the weight of the past and the dissatis-faction with the present isolate the characters. They all ponder their own lives, lose themselves in memories, and torment themselves by analyzing their bore-dom. Everyone in the Prozorov family and all their acquaintances have their own problems—problems that preoccupy them even in the company of others and, therefore, separate them from their fellow beings. Andrei is crushed by the discrepancy between a longed-for professorship in Moscow and his actual posi-tion as secretary to the rural district council. Masha married unhappily when she was seventeen. Olga believes that "in the four years [she has] been teaching at the school, [she has] felt [her] strength and youth draining away drop by drop."[5] And Irina, who has plunged into her work to overcome her dissatisfaction and sadness,[6] admits:

I'm going on twenty-four already; I've worked for years now and my brain's all dried up. I've grown old and thin and unattractive without having ever found anything the slightest bit satisfactory or rewarding and time goes by and I feel I'm going farther and farther away from a real, beautiful life, slipping down into some sort of an abyss. I've lost all hope and I don't even understand how it is that I'm still alive and haven't killed myself yet.[7]

The question is, then, how does this thematic renunciation of the present in favor of memory and longing, this perennial analysis of one's own fate, fit with a dra-matic form in which the Renaissance creed of the here and now, of the interper-sonal, was once crystallized? The double renunciation that marks Chekhov's characters seems inevitably to necessitate the abandonment of action and dialogue—the two most important formal categories of the Drama and, thus, dramatic form itself.

But one senses only a tendency in this direction. Despite their psychic ab-sence from social life, the heroes of Chekhov's plays live on. They do not draw any ultimate conclusions from their loneliness and longing. Instead, they hover midway between the world and the self, between now and then, so the formal presentation does not have to reject completely those categories necessary for it to be dramatic. They are maintained in a deemphasized, incidental manner that allows the real subject negative expression as a deviation from traditional dramatic form.

The Three Sisters does have the rudiments of traditional action. The first act, the exposition, takes place on Irina's name day. The second presents transitional events: Andrei's marriage, the birth of his son. The third takes place at night while a great fire rages in the neighborhood. The fourth presents the duel in which Irina's fiancé is killed—on the very day the regiment moves out of town, leaving the Prozorovs to succumb completely to the boredom of provincial life. This disconnected juxtaposition of active moments and their arrangement into four acts (which was, from the first, thought to lack tension) clearly reveals their place in the formal whole. They are included, although they do not actually express anything, to set the thematic in motion sufficiently to allow space for dialogue.

But even this dialogue carries no weight. It is the pale background on which monologic responses framed as conversation appear as touches of color in which the meaning of the whole is concentrated. These resigned self-analyses—which allow almost all the characters to make individual statements—give life to the work. It was written for their sake.

They are not monologues in the traditional sense of the word. Their source is not in the situation but in the subject. As G[eorg] Lukács has demonstrated, the dramatic monologue formulates nothing that cannot be communicated otherwise.[8] "Hamlet hides his feelings from the people at court for practical reasons. Perhaps, in fact, because they would all too readily understand that he wishes to take vengeance for his father—that he must take vengeance."[9] The situation is quite different in Chekhov's play. The lines are spoken aloud in front of others, not while alone, and they isolate the speaker. Thus, almost without notice, empty dialogue turns into substance-filled monologue. These are not isolated monologues built into a work structured around the dialogue. Rather it is through them that the work as a whole departs from the dramatic and becomes lyric. In lyric poetry, language is less in need of justification than in the Drama. It is, as it were, more formal. In the Drama, speech, in addition to conveying the concrete meaning of the words, also announces the fact that something is being spoken. When there is nothing more to say or when something cannot be expressed, the Drama is reduced to silence. In the lyric, on the other hand, silence speaks too. Of course words are no longer "exchanged" in the course of a conversation; instead, all is spoken with a naturalness that is inherent in the nature of the lyric.

This constant movement from conversation into the lyrics of loneliness is what gives Chekhov's language its charm. Its origins probably lie in Russian expansiveness and in the immanent lyric quality of the language itself. Loneliness is not the same thing as torpor here. What the Occidental most probably experiences only while intoxicated—participation in the loneliness of the other, the inclusion of individual loneliness in a growing collective loneliness—seems to be a possibility inherent in the Russian: the person and the language.

This is the reason the monologues in Chekhov's plays fit comfortably into the dialogue. It also explains why the dialogue creates so few problems in these plays and why the internal contradiction between monologic thematic and dialogic declaration does not lead to the destruction of the dramatic form.

Only Andrei, the three sisters' brother, is incapable of even this mode of expression. His loneliness forces him into silence; therefore, he avoids company.[10] He can speak only when he knows he will not be understood.

Chekhov manages this by making Ferapont, the watchman at the district council offices, hard of hearing.

> *Andrei*: How are you old friend? What can I do for you?
> *Ferapont*: The council chairman sends you a book and some papers.
> Here . . . (*Hands him a book and a packet.*)
> *Andrei*: Thanks, that's fine. But why did you come over so late? It's after eight already.
> *Ferapont*: What say?
> *Andrei* (*louder*): I said, you came over very late. It's after eight.
> *Ferapont*: That's right. It was still light when I got here, but they wouldn't let me in to see you. . . . (*Thinking Andrei has said something.*) What?
> *Andrei*: I didn't say a thing. (*Looks over the book.*) Tomorrow's Friday and I'm off, but I'll come over anyway and do some work. I get bored at home. (*Pauses.*) Ah, old fellow, how life changes; what tricks it plays on us! Today I had nothing to do so I picked up this book here—it's an old collection of university lectures—and I felt like laughing. Good lord, here I am, secretary of the Rural Council, the council, mind you, of which Protopopov is chairman, and the most I can hope for is to become a member one day. Imagine, me a member of the local council, when every night I dream that I'm a professor at Moscow University and a famous scholar of whom all Russia is proud!
> *Ferapont*: I wouldn't know . . . I don't hear so good.
> *Andrei*: It's just as well, because I hardly would've spoken to you like this if you could hear. I need someone to talk to, since my wife doesn't understand me and I'm afraid that my sisters would laugh in my face. . . . I don't like bars but let me tell you, old man, right now I'd give anything to be sitting at Testov's or in the Great Moscow Inn.
> *Ferapont*: And me, I heard some contractor over at the Council telling them that he'd seen some merchants in Moscow eating pancakes.

And there was one of 'em ate forty, and it seems he died. Either forty or fifty, I can't say for sure.

Andrei: You can go into a big Moscow restaurant where you don't know anyone and no one knows you, and yet you feel perfectly at home there. Now, here, you know everyone and everyone knows you, and yet you feel like a stranger among them. — And a lonely stranger at that.

Ferapont: What? (*Pause*.) Well, that same contractor was saying that they're stretching a big rope right across the whole of Moscow — but maybe he was lying at that![11]

Although this passage seems to be dialogue — thanks to the support given by the motif of not hearing — it is really a despairing monologue by Andrei. Ferapont provides counterpoint with his own equally monologic speech. Whereas elsewhere there is the possibility of real understanding because of a common subject, here its impossibility is expressed. The impression of divergence is greatest when the speeches simulate convergence. Andrei's monologue does not arise out of the dialogue. It comes from the negation of dialogue. The expressivity of this cross-purpose speaking is rooted in a painful, parodistic contrast with real dialogue, which it removes into the utopian. But dramatic form itself is called into question at this point.

Because the collapse of communication is motivated in *The Three Sisters* (Ferapont's inability to hear), a return to dialogue is still possible. Ferapont is only an occasional figure on stage. But everything thematic, the content of which is larger and weightier than the motif that serves to represent it, struggles toward precipitation as form. And the formal withdrawal of dialogue leads, of necessity, to the epic. Ferapont's inability to hear points the way to the future.

3. Strindberg

What was later called *I* dramaturgy, and shaped the image of dramatic literature for decades to come, actually began with Strindberg. In his case it was a dramaturgy rooted in autobiography. This is obvious in more than the thematic continuity of his plays. His theory of the "subjective drama" itself seems to coincide with that of the psychological novel (the history of the development of one's own soul) in his outline of the literature of the future. A comment made during an interview concerning the first volume of his autobiography, *The Son of a Servant*, also sheds light on the new dramatic style which emerged a year later with *The Father* (1887). He said:

I believe that the complete portrayal of an individual's life is truer and more meaningful than that of a whole family. How can one know what goes on in the minds of others, how can one be aware of the hidden reasons for someone else's deed, how can one know what one person has said to another in a moment of confidence? One makes suppositions, of course. But the study of the human species has not, up to now, been helped much by those authors who have used their limited psychological knowledge in an attempt to sketch the life of a soul, something that, in reality, remains hidden. One knows only *one* life, one's own.[1]

One could easily read into these lines, written in 1886, a rejection, pure and simple, of the dramatic. In fact, they present the basic preconditions for a developmental process which encompasses *The Father* (1887), *To Damascus* (1897–1904), *A Dream Play* (1901–02), and *The Great Highway* (1909). How far these developments actually lead away from the Drama is central to the problem of analyzing Strindberg's work.

The Father is an attempt to blend subjective and naturalist styles. The result is that neither could be fully realized because the goals of naturalist and subjective dramaturgy stood in radical opposition to each other. Naturalism, however revolutionary it was or wanted to be in style or "worldview," actually took a conservative position in questions of dramaturgy. Preservation of the traditional dramatic form was central to naturalism. Behind the revolutionary desire to give a new style to the Drama lay, as will be seen, the conservative idea of saving the Drama from intellectual-historical jeopardy by shifting it into a realm both archaic and contemporary, although untouched by recent developments.

At first glance, *The Father* seems to be a family drama similar to those countless others written at the time. The father and mother collide over the question of the daughter's upbringing: a struggle of principles; a battle of the sexes. But one does not need to keep in mind the remarks quoted above to see that the work is not a direct, that is, dramatic, presentation of this poisoned relationship and its history. It is constructed solely from the standpoint of the title figure and unfolds through his subjective point of view. An outline of the play only hints at this: the father is in the middle, surrounded by women—Laura, his nurse, the mother-in-law, and, finally, the daughter—who form the walls of the female hell in which he believes himself to be. More important is the recognition that the battle waged against him by his wife usually achieves "dramatic" realization only as a reflection of his own consciousness. Its main features are even established by him. He himself hands over to his wife her most important weapon—the question of paternity. And his mental illness is attested to by one of his own letters, in which he "feared for his sanity."[2] The lines his wife speaks at the end of the second act, which lead him to throw the burning lamp at her, are believable only as a projection of the thoughts the Captain himself suspects his wife of having. "Now you have fulfilled your destiny as a father and family supporter. . . . You are no longer needed . . . and so you must go!" If naturalist dialogue is an exact reproduction of conversation as it might take place in reality, Strindberg's first "naturalist" work is as much at odds with it as is the *tragédie classique*. They differ in their *principium stilisationis*. The neoclassical Drama posits its principle as an objective ideal. In *The Father* it is determined by the subjective perspective. The Captain's fall, which Laura prepares with the straitjacket, is transformed into a profoundly internal process because of its connection with his childhood and because of his magico-psychoanalytic identification with the memories contained in the words the nursemaid speaks as she puts him into the jacket.

Because of this displacement, the three unities, which are rigorously observed in *The Father*, become meaningless. Their function in genuine Drama is to raise the purely dialectical-dynamic flow of events above the static situation caused by the isolation of internal and external worlds, thereby creating that absolute space which the exclusive reproduction of interpersonal events requires.[3] This play, however, depends on the unity of the *I* of its central figure, not on that of action. The unity of action is not essential to the presentation of psychic development and may even interfere with it. There is no need for a flawless action, and there is no necessary correlation between the unities of time and place and that of the psyche. That much is made clear in the few scenes in which the Captain is not on stage. There seems to be no real reason why the spectator, who sees the family's reality through the father's eyes, should not follow him on his nightly walks and, later, be locked in with him. To be sure, even the scenes from which he is absent are dominated by him. He is present as the sole subject of conversation. Laura's intrigues are only indirectly visible; in the foreground stands the picture she paints of him for her brother and the Doctor. And when the Pastor learns of his sister's plan to hospitalize the Captain and have him judged incompetent, he becomes the spokesman for his brother-in-law—a man he had otherwise always "regarded . . . as a weed in our family pasture,"[4] because of his free thinking.

> You are a strong woman, Laura! Unbelievably strong! Like a fox in a trap, you would rather gnaw off your leg than allow yourself to be caught! Like a master thief, you have no accomplice—not even your own conscience! Look at yourself in the mirror! You don't dare! . . . Let me look at your hand! Not a sign of blood to betray you—not a trace of insidious poison! An innocent murder that cannot be reached by the law—an unconscious crime—unconscious mind you! A clever scheme, a master stroke![5]

And speaking for himself instead of for his brother-in-law, the Pastor concludes, "As a man, I would gladly see you hung! As brother and as pastor, my compliments."* But even these final words echo those spoken by the Captain.

These few points, all of which show the growing problems of character portrayal and the unities in the realm of subjective drama, indicate why Strindberg's naturalist and autobiographical intentions go their separate ways after *The Father*. *Miss Julie*, written a year later and not conceived in perspective, became one of the most famous of all naturalist plays and Strindberg's foreword to it, a kind of naturalist manifesto.

His efforts to place the ego of a single individual, primarily his own, at the center of a work led further and further away from traditional dramatic construction, however (*Miss Julie* had remained fully within this tradition). First came experiments in monodrama, such as *The Stronger*. That seems to be a logical result of the idea that one can know only "*one* life, one's own." It should be added, though, that the single role in this play is not an autobiographical portrait of Strindberg. This is understandable when one remembers that subjective theater arises less out of the notion that one can describe only one's own psychic existence (since it is all one can know) than from the prior intention of bringing this mostly secret psychic existence to life dramatically. The Drama, the art form par excellence of dialogic openness and frankness, is given the task of presenting secret psychic events. It accomplishes this first by withdrawing into the central figure and then by either limiting itself to this character (monodrama) or enclosing the others within the character's frame of reference (*I*-dramaturgy). At which point it ceases to be Drama, of course.

The one-act *The Stronger* (1888–89) is probably more important in relation to the inner problematic of the modern analytical technique in general than it is to Strindberg's dramatic development in particular. It should, in this case, be looked at in terms of Ibsen's work, since in this monodrama of six pages can be found something akin to the core of the three—or four—act play by Ibsen. The secondary action, the one in the present, which serves as a backdrop for the primary action exists only in embryo: "On Christmas night, Mrs. X, actress, married," meets "Miss Y, actress, unmarried," at a corner table in a tea house. And the internal reflexes, the memories of the past—which Ibsen intertwines dramatically in such a masterful yet dubious fashion with actual events—is presented here by the married actress in a grand epic-lyric monologue. At this point one sees more clearly how undramatic Ibsen's material was and the price Ibsen had to pay because he held fast to dramatic form. The hidden and the repressed appear with incomparably greater power in the density and purity of Strindberg's monologue than in Ibsen's dialogue. And their revelation does not require that "unparalleled act of violence" which Rilke saw in Ibsen's work.[6] Far from turning into mere reportage, this self-narration even manages to produce two peripeteias that could hardly be more "dramatic," despite the fact that, because of their pure interiority, they move beyond dialogue and, therefore, beyond the Drama as well.

In 1897, after a five-year pause in his work, Strindberg created his own form, the "station drama," with *To Damascus*. Fourteen shorter pieces from the years

1887–92 and the long hiatus between the years 1893–97 separate this play from his major work *The Father*. The one-acts from this period (eleven in all, counting *The Stronger*) push into the background the problems of dramatic action and role construction that appear in *The Father*. They do not solve these problems; instead, they bear indirect witness to them—through their efforts to avoid them.

The "station drama," on the other hand, provided a formal equivalent to the thematic intent of that subjective theater which *The Father* had already hinted at. The internal contradiction that subjective dramaturgy had created within the dramatic form was, therefore, eliminated. The subjective dramatist is most concerned with the isolation and elevation of a central figure who most often represents the dramatist himself. The dramatic form, the basis of which is a constantly renewed balance in personal interplay, cannot satisfy the subjective dramatist without destroying itself. In the "station drama," the hero, whose development is described, is separated in the clearest possible manner from the other figures he meets at the stations along his way. They appear only in terms of his encounters with them and only from his perspective. They are, thus, references to him. And because the "station drama" is not constructed around a number of more or less equally important characters but, rather, around a central *I*, its space is not a priori dialogic; the monologue loses the exceptional quality it necessarily has in the Drama. And the limitless unfolding of a "secret psychic existence" becomes formally possible.

Subjective theater also leads to the replacement of the unity of action by the unity of the self. The station technique accounts for this change by replacing continuity of action with a series of scenes. These individual scenes stand in no causal relationship and do not, as in the Drama, generate one another. On the contrary, they seem to be isolated stones strung out along the path of the onward moving *I*. This static, futureless quality of the scenes (which makes them, in Goethe's sense of the word, epic) is tied to a structure that is defined by the perspective from which the self faces the world. The dynamics of the dramatic scene arise out of an interpersonal dialectic. The scene is driven forward because of the future moment contained in this dialectic. In the "station drama," on the other hand, there is no mutual rapport. The hero does encounter other people, but they remain strangers.

When this happens the very possibility of dialogue is called into question and, in his last "station drama" (*The Great Highway*), Strindberg, in certain places, actually shifted from a dialogic structure to that of an epic for two voices:

> *The Hunter and the Wanderer are seated at a table, outside, each one with a glass before him.*
>
> *Wanderer*: It's peaceful down here in the valley.
> *Hunter*: A little too peaceful, thinks the miller . . .

Wanderer: . . . who sleeps, no matter how hard the water runs . . .
Hunter: . . . because he is always on the alert for wind and weather . . .
Wanderer: . . . which useless pursuit has awakened in me a certain
   antipathy to windmills . . .
Hunter: . . . just as it did in the noble knight Don Quixote of la
   Mancha . . .
Wanderer: . . . who never, however, became a turncoat because of
   the way the wind blew . . .
Hunter: . . . but rather the opposite . . .
Wanderer: . . . which is the reason for his getting into perplexing sit-
   uations. . . . [7]

This kind of scene cannot provide a transition into another scene. Only the
hero can internalize and take with him its traumatic or healing effects. The scene
itself is left behind as a station along his way.

When a subjective path replaces objective action in this manner, the unities
of time and place cease to be valid categories. This has to be the case, since only
isolated turns along a basically internal pathway are presented on stage. In the
"station drama," this pathway is not, as is the action in genuine Drama, shown
in its entirety. The hero's development continues between times and between
places and, thus, by constantly going beyond the objective boundaries of the
work, makes it relative.

Because organic rapport does not exist between the individual scenes and because they represent only segments of a development that extends beyond the
work (they are, so to speak, scenic fragments from an *Entwicklungsroman*),
their composition can arise even out of an external schema that further
relativizes the scenes and makes them more epic. Unlike the dramatic model
constructed by G[ustav] Freytag, in which the pyramid he postulates arises of
necessity out of the organic growth of the acts and scenes, the symmetric construction of *To Damascus I* follows a mechanical pattern of organization which,
although understandable, is alien to the work.

By presenting the interpersonal as a harsh juxtaposition, the "station drama"
seems to contradict Strindberg's "expressionism," according to which the characters, as in the *Damascus* trilogy (the Lady, the Beggar, Caesar), are projections
of the Stranger's own psyche, and the work as a whole, therefore, is located in
the subjectivity of its hero.[8] But this contradiction represents the paradox of subjectivity itself: self-alienation in reflections, the reification of the self through
self-contemplation, the sudden transformation of energized subjectivity into the
objective. It is quite clear in psychoanalytic terminology that the conscious *I*
(that is, the *I* as it becomes aware of itself) views the unconscious as a stranger.
The unconscious appears as the id [it]. Thus, the isolated individual, fleeing
from the world into himself, is confronted once again by someone unknown.
The Stranger recognizes this at the outset of the play.

I have no fear of death. It is loneliness I am afraid of—for the loneliness of life is peopled. . . . I don't know whether it is someone else or myself I sense—but in loneliness one is never alone. The air becomes dense, the atmosphere thickens, and spirits that are invisible and yet have life can be perceived, hovering about.[9]

He meets these beings in what follows at the stations along his way. They are usually himself and a stranger at the same time; they seem most alien when they are himself. This meeting between two aspects of the self leads once more to the abolition of dialogue. The Lady in the *Damascus* trilogy, who is apparently a projection of the Stranger, can tell him only what he already knows.

Lady [*To the Mother*]: He is a little eccentric; and there is one thing I find rather tiresome: I can never mention anything that he doesn't already know. As a consequence we say very little to each other.[10]

The relationship between the subjective and the objective manifests itself temporally as a rapport between the present and the past. In thought, the remembered, internalized past reappears as an alien present: the others whom the stranger meets are often signs of his own past. Thus, the Doctor is a reference to a childhood schoolmate who, though innocent, was punished in his stead. The meeting with the Doctor objectifies in the present the source of the mental anguish which had never left him since that moment (a motif from Strindberg's own past). And the Beggar he meets on a street corner bears the scar he himself carries as a result of the blow he once received from his brother.

The "station drama" and Ibsen's analytical technique converge here. But, like the self-alienation of the isolated individual, the alienation of an individual's past acquires adequate form without dramaturgic "violence" in the separate encounters which compose Strindberg's work.

The meeting of the isolated *I* and the alienated-reified world is the foundation for the formal structure of two later works by Strindberg: *A Dream Play* (1901–2) and *The Ghost Sonata* (1907).

A Dream Play, written the same year as *To Damascus III*, does not differ from the "station drama" as far as its formal conception is concerned ([It reproduces] "the detached and disunited, although apparently logical, form of dreams"—Strindberg's preface). Strindberg also referred to *To Damascus* as a dream play, which is to say that he did not conceive of *A Dream Play* as an enacted dream. He used this title only to indicate the dreamlike composition of the work. Indeed, dream and "station drama" are alike in structure: a sequence of scenes whose unity does not reside in the action but in the unchanging psyche of the dreamer, who is, perhaps, the hero.

If the emphasis is on the self in isolation in the "station drama," in *A Dream Play*, it is the world of human activity that stands in the foreground as an object of observation for the god Indra's Daughter. This is the notion that constitutes the play and that determines its form—Indra's Daughter is shown "what human life is like" (Strindberg). The loosely connected scenes in *A Dream Play* are more like those of a revue from the Middle Ages than those of a dream. And the revue is—in opposition to the Drama—essentially a presentation that unfolds for someone who is not part of it. Because of this, *A Dream Play*, in which the observer is the real *I* of the play, has the epic structure of a confrontation between subject and object.

Indra's Daughter, who in the original version (without prologue) seems to be a dramatis persona coequal with the others, formulates her epic separation from mankind in her leitmotivlike remark, "human beings are pitiful." The content of the remark indicates pity; formally, however, it expresses distance and can, therefore, become the magic phrase through which Indra's Daughter, even during her deepest involvement (in Strindberg's eyes) in things human—her marriage to the Lawyer—can rise above human existence.

> *Daughter*: I am beginning to hate you after all this.
> *Lawyer*: Alas for us then! But let us prevent hatred. I promise never to mention untidiness again, although it is torture to me.
> *Daughter*: And I will eat cabbage, although that is a torment to me.
> *Lawyer*: And so—life together is a torment. One's pleasure is the other's pain.
> *Daughter*: Human beings are pitiful.[11]

In accord with its revuelike structure, the work's most characteristic gesture is that of showing. In addition to the Officer (who represents Strindberg), the figures Indra's Daughter encounters are primarily those who have, as it were, a concrete sense of mankind because of their professions and can, therefore, serve best to present it. Thus, for example, the Lawyer (the second incarnation of the author) says:

> *Lawyer*: Look at these walls! Isn't the wallpaper stained as if by every kind of sin? Look at these documents in which I write records of evil! Look at me! . . . Nobody who comes here ever smiles. Nothing but vile looks, bared teeth, clenched fists, and all of them squirt their malice, their envy, their suspicions over me. Look my hands are black and can never be clean! See how cracked they are and bleeding! I can never wear my clothes for more than a few days because they stink of other people's crimes. . . . Look at me! Do you think, marked as I am by crime, I can ever win a woman's love? Or that anyone wants to be the friend of a man who has to enforce payment of all the debts in town? It's misery to be human.
> *Daughter*: Human life is pitiable.[12]

The Poet (Strindberg's third incarnation) hands Indra's Daughter a "petition from mankind to the ruler of the universe, drawn up by a dreamer,"[13] which has as its subject the *condition humaine*. He also shows her this condition as embodied in another human being.

Enter Lina with a bucket.

Poet: Lina, show yourself to Miss Agnes [Indra's Daughter]. She knew you ten years ago when you were a young, happy, and, let me add, pretty girl. . . . Look at her now! Five children, drudgery, squalling, hunger, blows. See how beauty has perished, how joy has vanished in the fulfillment of duties.[14]

The Officer, too, occasionally takes an epic stance.

An elderly man walks past with his hands behind his back.
Officer: Look, there goes a pensioner waiting for his life to ebb. A captain probably, who failed to become a Major, or a Clerk to the Court who was never promoted. Many are called, but few are chosen. He's just walking about waiting for breakfast.
Pensioner: No, for the paper, the morning paper!
Officer: And he's only fifty-four. He may go on for another twenty-five years, waiting for meals and the newspaper. Isn't that dreadful?[15]

In other words, *A Dream Play* is in no way a work in which mankind enacts itself — a Drama — rather, it is an epic play *about* mankind. This presentational structure (although hidden both thematically and formally) defines the *Ghost Sonata* as well. In *A Dream Play*, the structure manifests itself thematically in the visit Indra's Daughter makes to earth and formally in the revue style arrangements of the scenes. In the *Ghost Sonata*, on the other hand, the structure is hidden behind the facade of a traditional salon Drama. It is not used as an all-encompassing formal principle. Instead, it functions as a means of achieving certain ends; for the *Ghost Sonata* presents the same formal problem that Ibsen's late work did: how to reveal dramatically a secret and deeply internalized past, how to prevent it from escaping dramatic presentation. In Ibsen's work discovery is made possible by intertwining the past with a topical dramatic action; in Strindberg's one-act *The Stronger*, by the use of monologue. In the *Ghost Sonata*, both these methods are employed to a certain degree — the monologic *I* of subjective theater appears in the midst of the other characters dressed as an ordinary dramatis persona. It will be this character's function to unroll the secret past of the others. This role belongs to the old man, Hummel. Through him, as through the Lawyer and the Poet in *A Dream Play*, mankind is seen as an object, from the outside. In response to the Student's opening question, — whether Hummel knows the people "who live there" (that is, the people Hummel will later unmask), he answers, "Every one of them. At my age one knows everybody . . . but no one knows me—not really. I take an interest in human destiny."[16] Just as this line gives a thematic basis for Hummel's formal role and special position, so do the following statements explain why these people need an epic narrator.

> Bengston (*The butler in the house* [*a figure parallel to Hummel*] *describes his employers to Hummels attendant*): The usual ghost supper, as we call it. They drink tea and don't say a word—or else the Colonel does all the talking. . . . And they've kept this up for twenty years, and always the same people saying the same things or saying nothing at all for fear of being found out.[17]

And in the third act:

> *Student*: . . . Tell me. Why do your parents sit in there so silently, not saying a single word?
> *Girl*: Because they have nothing to say to each other, and because neither believes what the other says. This is how my father puts it: What's the point of talking, when neither of us can fool the other?[18]

These lines mark one source of modern epic dramaturgy. They locate the moment when middle-class salon Drama, which had taken over the formal principles of the neoclassical Drama, was transformed, of necessity, into the epic because of the form-content contradiction that had arisen in the course of the nineteenth century. Within this process, Hummel's presence may well be the first example of the epic *I* appearing on stage, albeit disguised as an ordinary dramatic character. In the first act, he describes the inhabitants of the house to the Student. Devoid of all dramatic independence, they show themselves at the windows—objects to be presented. In the second act, during the ghost supper, it is Hummel who unmasks their secrets.

It is difficult to understand, however, why Strindberg remained unaware of this character's formal function. In the second act, he lets the traditional unmasking of the unmasker end in Hummel's suicide. The work thereby loses, on the level of its content, the formal principle on which it was built. The third act had to fail, because, with no epic support, it could not generate dialogue of its own. In addition to the episodic figure of the Cook, who, surprisingly enough, carries on Hummel's thematic "vampire" role without taking over his formal role, the Girl and the Student are the only characters capable of carrying a dialogue, but they can no longer sufficiently free themselves from the spell of the ghost house to create one. Their desperate, wandering conversation—interrupted by pauses, monologues, and prayers—ends the play. This tormenting, failed conclusion to a unique work can be understood only in terms of the transitional dramaturgic situation to which it belongs. The epic structure is there but still thematically bound and, thus, subject to the unfolding of the action.

Whereas in Ibsen's plays the dramatis personae had to die because they had no epic narrator, Strindberg's first stage narrator dies because he is not recognized as such—he wears the mask of a dramatis persona. More than anything else, this demonstrates the internal contradictions in the Drama at the turn of the century and precisely designates Ibsen's and Strindberg's historical position. The former comes just before, the latter just after the sublation of these contradictions via a conversion of the thematic epic into epic form. Both, then, are on the threshold of that modern theater which can be understood only in terms of *its own* form problematic.

4. Maeterlinck

Maeterlinck's early work (it alone will be discussed here) is an attempt to dramatize existential powerlessness—mankind's dependence on a fate that is forever obscure. Greek tragedy depicted the hero in conflict with destiny. Neoclassical Drama displayed the conflicts arising from interpersonal relationships. In Maeterlinck's work only a single moment is dealt with—the moment when a helpless human being is overtaken by fate. Not in the manner in which this took place in the romantic *Schicksalstragödie*, however; it focused on human interaction within the sphere of a fate that was blind. The mechanics of destiny unfolding and a concomitant perversion of human relations were its themes. There is none of this in Maeterlinck's plays. For him, human destiny is represented by death itself, and death alone dominates the stage in his works. But not as any particular figure, not in any particular tragic connection with life; no action brings on death, no one is responsible for it. From the dramaturgic point of view, this means that the category "action" is replaced by "situation." The genre Maeterlinck created should, in fact, bear this name, because the essential in each of these plays does not reside in the action. They are, therefore, no longer "Dramas"—as long as the Greek word is understood in this sense. It is this distinction that lies behind the rather paradoxical term *drame statique*, which Maeterlinck coined for his work.

In genuine Drama, situation is only the starting point for the action. In the *drame statique*, on the other hand, the possibility of human action has been eliminated for thematic reasons. The individual waits in total passivity until death's presence penetrates his consciousness. Only the attempt to verify his situation permits the individual to speak. When he becomes aware of death (the demise of someone close to him), which, because of his blindness, he has not seen standing in front of him the whole time, he has reached his goal. This is the subject of *L'intruse, Les aveugles* (both published in 1890), and *Interieur* (1894).

The stage, as set for *Les aveugles* [*The Blind*], presents an "ancient Norland forest, with an eternal look, under a sky of deep stars. — In the centre and in the deep of the night, a very old priest is sitting wrapped in a great black cloak. The chest and the head, gently upturned and deathly motionless, rest against the trunk of a giant hollow oak. The face is terribly pale and of an immovable waxen lividness, in which purple lips fall slightly apart. The dumb, fixed eyes no longer look out from the visible side of eternity and seem to bleed with immemorial sorrows and with tears. . . . On the right, six old men, all blind, are sitting on stones, stumps and dead leaves. — On the left, separated from them by an uprooted tree and fragments of rock, six women, also blind, are sitting opposite the old men. . . . It is unusually oppressive, despite the moonlight that here and there struggles to pierce for an instant the gloom of the foliage."[1] The blind figures are waiting for the return of the old priest who led them to this place, and he is sitting in their midst — dead.

Even the detailed stage directions, which have been quoted only in part here, show that the dialogic form is insufficient as a means of presentation. Or vice versa — what there is to say is an insufficient basis on which to build a dialogue. The twelve blind characters pose anxious questions about their fate and thereby slowly become aware of their situation. Conversation is thus limited and its rhythm determined by the exchange of question and answer.

> *First Blind Man* (*blind from birth*): He hasn't come yet?
> *Second Blind Man* (*also born blind*): I hear nothing coming.[2]

Later:

> *Second Blind Man*: Are we in the sun now?
> *Third Blind Man* (*also born blind*): Is the sun still shining?[3]

Often the statements move parallel to one another and sometimes even at cross-purposes.

> *Third Blind Man*: It's time to go back to the home.
> *First Blind Man*: We ought to find out where we are.
> *Second Blind Man*: It has grown cold since we left.[4]

Whatever symbolic content blindness may have, dramaturgically it saves the work from the silence that threatens it. It represents human powerlessness and isolation ("Years and years we have been together, and we have never seen each other! You would say we were forever alone. . . . To love one must see.")[5]* and, therefore, calls into question the possibility of dialogue. At the same time, it is solely due to this blindness that there is still cause for speech. In *L'intruse*, which presents a family gathered together while the Mother lies dying in the next room, it is the blind Grandfather whose questions (and premonitions, since as a blind person he sees both less and more than the others) generate the conversation.

The verbal exchanges in *Les aveugles* move away from dialogue in several directions. They are mainly choral. The little individualization granted the twelve blind figures is lost in the responses in this play. Language cuts itself free; its essentially dramatic ties to position disappear. It is no longer the expression of an individual awaiting a response; instead, language expresses the mood that reigns in all the characters' souls. The fact that this language is divided into individual lines in no way makes it synonymous with the conversation in genuine Drama. It simply reflects the nervous glitter of uncertainty. It can be read or heard without paying attention to who is speaking. The essential is the language's intermittence, not its relation to an immediate *I*. This means that the dramatis personae are far from being causal agents or subjects of an action. They are, quite simply, objects of an action. This single theme in Maeterlinck's early work—the individual, helpless in the face of destiny—calls for an equivalent formal statement.

The manner in which he conceived *Interieur* shows the results of this need. In it, too, a family experiences death. The daughter, who left in the morning to look for her grandmother on the other side of the river, drowned herself, and her body is brought back to the house. Her parents are not expecting her yet and are passing a calm, carefree evening. Just as these five people (to whom death comes unexpectedly) are speechless victims of destiny, so, too, they formally become the mute epic objects of the person who has come to inform them of the daughter's death. The Old Man, before he undertakes this difficult task, talks to a stranger about them in front of a brightly lit window through which the family is visible. Thus, the body of the drama is split in two—into the mute characters in the house and those in the garden who speak. This division into thematic and dramaturgic groups illustrates a subject-object separation which turns human beings into objects and which is fundamental to Maeterlinck's fatalism. It creates an epic situation inside the Drama, which had been possible only occasionally before—in descriptions of offstage battles, for example. Here, however, it forms the whole of the work. The "dialogue" between the Stranger, the Old Man, and his two grandchildren serves almost entirely as an epic description of the silent family.

The Old Man: I would like to see, first, if they are all in the room. Yes, I see the father sitting in the chimney-corner. He waits with his hands on his knees; . . . the mother is resting her elbow on the table.[6]

There is even a certain amount of awareness of the epic distance, which arises because the narrator knows more than the objects of his narration.

The Old Man: I am nearly eighty-three years old, and this is the first time the sight of life has struck me. I don't know why everything they do seems so strange and grave to me. . . . They wait for night quite simply, under their lamp, as we might have been wait- ing under ours; and yet I seem to see them from the height of an- other world, because I know a little truth which they don't know yet.[7]

Even the most animated conversation is really only description that has been divided up between the speakers.

The Stranger: Just now they are smiling in silence in the room . . .
The Old Man: They are at peace . . . they did not expect her tonight . . .
The Stranger: They smile without stirring, . . . and see, the father is putting his finger on his lips.
The Old Man: He is calling attention to the child asleep on its mother's heart.
The Stranger: She dares not raise her eyes lest she disturb its sleep.[8]

Maeterlinck's decision to dramatize the human situation as he saw it led him to present his characters as silent, suffering objects in the hands of death. He did this within a form that, until then, had known only speaking, active subjects. This caused a shift toward the epic within the concept of the Drama itself. In *Les aveugles*, the characters describe their own situation—their blindness is sufficient motivation. In *Interieur*, the hidden epic element in the material is even more evident. It creates an actual narrative situation in which subject and object stand facing each other. But even this remains thematic and requires fur- ther motivation inside a now meaningless dramatic form.

5. Hauptmann

What was said previously in reference to Ibsen is, in part, also valid for Haupt- mann's early work; *Das Friedensfest* (1890), for example, is a typical "analytical drama." It lays out the history of a family on a Christmas evening. But even Hauptmann's first play, *Before Sunrise* (1889), contains a perspective not found in Ibsen's work. The play's subtitle, *A Social Drama*, announces the difference. Critics have usually accounted for this difference by concluding that Hauptmann had had another teacher as well: Tolstoy and his play *The Power of Darkness*. However powerful Tolstoy's influence might have been, an analysis of the inter- nal problems of Hauptmann's "social Drama" has to be carried out without refer- ence to it, because Tolstoy's play poses none of the sociological-naturalistic problems found in Hauptmann's work. Furthermore, Tolstoy overcomes the for- mal difficulties of the Drama through the same Russian lyric tendency found in Chekhov's plays.

The social dramatist attempts to dramatize the politico-economic structures which dictate the conditions of individual life. He has to show factors that are larger than those of a single situation or a single action—factors which, nonetheless, define such situations and actions. This kind of dramatic presentation requires another sort of work first: the transformation of alienated conditionality into interpersonal actuality;* in other words, the conversion and dispersal of historical process in the aesthetic realm that is supposed to reflect it. The dubiousness of this attempt becomes absolutely clear when one looks closely at the manner in which form evolves in this case. Transforming alienated conditionality into interpersonal actuality means finding an action that will give presence to these states. This action, which functions as a subsidiary mediating between the social thematic and the preexisting dramatic form, proves to be problematic from the standpoint of the thematic as well as of form. An action which represents is not dramatic: the events in the Drama, absolute in themselves, can stand for nothing beyond themselves. Even in the philosophical tragedies of Kleist or Hebbel, the plot has no demonstrative function. It is not "meaningful" in the sense that it points beyond itself to the nature of the universe as conceived by the author in a personal metaphysics. Instead, it focuses on itself and its own metaphysical depths. This in no way limits its capacity to make meaningful statements—quite the contrary: the world of the Drama can, because of its absoluteness, stand for the real world. The relationship between signifier and signified resides in the symbolic principle that unites microcosm-macrocosm but not in the *pars pro toto*. But this is precisely what is found in the "social Drama." In every sense it works against the requisite absoluteness in dramatic form: the dramatis personae represent thousands of people living in the same conditions; their situation represents a uniformity determined by economic factors. Their fate is an example, a means of "showing" that implies not only an objectivity which transcends the work but also a subject which stands above the play and does the showing: the authorial *I*. In the work of art, tension between the empirical and creative subjectivity—open reference to something external to the work—is the formal basis for the epic, not the Drama. The "social Drama" is, therefore, epic in nature and a contradiction in itself.

However, the transformation of alienated conditionality into interpersonal actuality also contradicts the thematic intention itself. Its goal is to show that the determinant forces in human existence have been transferred from the sphere of the "interpersonal" to that of alienated objectivity; that, fundamentally speaking, there is no present—so much does it resemble what has always been and will be; that an action which outlines the present and thus lays the basis for a new future is impossible as long as these crippling forces hold sway.

Hauptmann tried to resolve the problematics of the social drama in *Before Sunrise* and *The Weavers*. *Before Sunrise* undertakes the description of those Silesian farmers who, having become wealthy because of the coal discovered under their fields, through idleness drift into a licentious and diseased way of life.

A typical example is chosen from this group—the farmer, Krause, and his family. He passes his days in drunkenness, while his wife has an affair with the fiancé of his daughter from a previous marriage. Martha, the eldest daughter, married to an engineer, Hoffmann, and about to give birth, has also become an alcoholic. Such characters cannot found a dramatic action. The vice into which they have sunk places them beyond interpersonal relationships. It isolates and debases them to speechless, screeching, vegetating animals. The only person in the family who is active, Krause's son-in-law, accommodates himself to the family's decadence and tries to exploit it and the neighborhood as well in whatever ways he can. But thereby, he too escapes the open, decision-filled present demanded by the Drama. And the life of the only pure individual in this family, the youngest daughter, Helene, is one of quiet, misunderstood suffering.

The dramatic action that is to present this family must, therefore, have its source outside the family. It must also be an action that leaves these characters in their thinglike objectivity and must not falsify the monotone, timeless quality of their being through a formally determined, taut development. Furthermore, this action has to expose the condition of the Silesian "coal farmers" as a whole.

This explains why a stranger, Alfred Loth, is brought into the play. A social researcher and childhood friend of Hoffmann's, he visits the region to study the situation of the miners. Thus, the Krause family is given dramatic presentation by gradually being revealed to the visitor. The reader or spectator sees the family from Loth's perspective—as an object of scientific research. In other words, Loth's role is a mask worn by the epic *I*. The dramatic action itself is none other than a thematic travesty of the formal principles of the epic: Loth's visit to the family reproduces thematically that movement of the epic narrator toward his object, which is the formal basis of the epic.

This happens more than once in the plays written at the turn of the century. The presence of a stranger whose appearance motivates the action is one of the more commonly observed characteristics of these works. Most critics, however, fail to see the conditions that necessitate his appearance and assign him a function parallel to that of the classical *raisonneur*. They have nothing in common though. Of course the stranger reasons, but the *raisonneur*, who could have freed him from the stain of the modern, was no outsider; he was part of the society which, through him, achieved ultimate transparency. The appearance of a stranger, on the other hand, expresses the incapacity of the characters to whom his presence gives dramatic life to achieve this life on their own. His mere presence is a sign of the crises in the Drama, and the Drama he makes possible is no longer really Drama. It has its roots in an epic subject-object relationship in which the stranger stands facing the others. The action unfolds because of the steps taken by an outsider; it is not determined by interpersonal conflict. Dramatic tension disappears. This is the basic problem with *Before Sunrise*. External tensions, the nerve-racking wait for Frau Hoffmann to give birth, for example, have to stand in for real tensions anchored in interpersonal relationships. Even the audience attending the première noticed the extra-artistic and the contingent nature of these practices. From the midst of the spectators, according to one well-known anecdote, a gynecologist raised his forceps aloft, no doubt as a sign that he wanted to offer his help.

Another undramatic element is added when the stranger appears. Real dramatic action does not present human existence in terms of some specific cause. If it did, the action would point beyond itself. Its presence is pure actuality, not the making present of a conditioned being. The existence of the dramatis personae should not reach beyond the temporal borders of the Drama. The notion of causation is, on the contrary, intelligible only within a temporal context, and, as an artistic means, it belongs to the epic and epic theater as it existed in the Middle Ages and the baroque period. There the thematic occasion corresponded (on the level of form) with the fact of the performance, a fact excluded from the Drama. Here, on the other hand, the play is openly announced as a play and refers to the actors and spectators. *Before Sunrise* shows none of this in its form, though. It takes up the epic principle itself as its plot line but retains a dramatic style that can be no more than partially successful.

Even the end of the play, which has always been considered incomprehensible and a failure, can be explained in this light. Loth, who is in love with Helene and wants to save her from the swamp in which she lives, leaves her and flees from the family when he learns of their inherited alcoholism. Helene, who had seen in Loth her only chance to escape, commits suicide. Loth's "loveless and cowardly dogmatism" has never been understood, especially because the spectator, without ever having grasped his formal function as onstage epic narrator, connects Loth with Hauptmann himself. The role was determined by the form, though. What distorts Loth's character at the end is the result of his formal, not his thematic, function. Just as the formal movement of the classic comedy requires that the maze of obstacles that hinders the lovers' engagement be overcome before the final curtain falls, so does the form of a Drama dependent on the arrival of a stranger require his departure from the stage at the close of the last act.

Thus the same thing occurs in *Before Dawn* that happens in the *Ghost Sonata* with Hummel's suicide, but in reverse. During this period of crisis in the Drama, epic formal elements appeared in thematic guise. The result of this doubling in the function of a role or a situation can be a collision between form and content. And if a content-bound event in the *Ghost Sonata* destroyed its hidden formal principle, here, in contrast, a formal requirement causes the action to slide into the incomprehensible.

Two years later (1891), Hauptmann completed his other "social drama," *The Weavers*. It is supposed to show the suffering of the weavers in the Eulen mountains in the mid-nineteenth century. The source of the work—as Hauptmann writes in his dedication—was his father's "story of grandfather, who when young sat at the loom, a poor weaver like those depicted here." These lines have been quoted because they also lead into the formal problems of the work. At its origin is an indelible image: weavers behind their looms and the knowledge of their misery. This seems to call for a figurative presentation, like that in the *Weavers' Uprising* cycle, which Kathe Kollwitz completed around 1897—inspired by Hauptmann, to be sure. For a dramatic presentation, however, the same question must be posed here about the possibility of dramatic action that was raised in relation to *Before Dawn*. Neither the life of the weavers, who have known only work and hunger, nor the political-economic situation can be transformed into dramatic actuality. The only action possible, given the conditions of their existence, is one *against* these conditions: an uprising. Hauptmann attempts to present the weavers' uprising of 1844. As motivation for the revolt, an epic description of conditions seems susceptible to dramatization. But the action itself is not dramatic. The weavers' uprising, with the exception of one scene in the last act, lacks interpersonal conflict. It does not develop through the medium of the dialogue (as does, for example, Schiller's *Wallenstein*) but rather from an explosion in people whose despair is beyond dialogue—an explosion that can at most become thematic material for some other dialogic exchange. Thus, the work becomes epic once more. It is constructed of scenes in which various elements of epic theater are used. This means that the relationship narrator-object is built thematically into the scenes.

The first act opens in Peterswaldau. The weavers are turning in their finished webs at the home of the manufacturer Dreissiger. The scene reminds one of a medieval revue, except that the introduction of the weavers and their misery is thematically motivated by the delivery of their work: the weavers present themselves along with their wares. The second act depicts the cramped room of a weaver family in Kaschbach. Their misery is described to an outsider, Moritz Jäger, who after long years of service as a soldier is estranged from the home-town to which he has returned. But it is precisely as an outsider—someone who has not succumbed to the living conditions there—that he is able to spark the fire of rebellion. The third act again takes place in Peterswaldau. It is set in the inn, where recent events are reported and discussed from time to time. And so the weavers' situation is first discussed by the local craftsmen, then further described by a second outsider, the Commercial Traveler. The fourth act, in Dreissiger's house, brings (after another dialogue *about* the weavers) the first dramatic scenes of the work. The fifth act, finally, takes one to Langenbielau and into the workroom at Old Hilse's. Here the events that have transpired in Peterswaldau are described. Then, in addition to a description of what is happening in the street (in the meantime the rebels have arrived in Langenbielau), comes the closing dramatic scene—the dispute between Old Hilse (who, having turned away from the events of this world, refuses to participate in the uprising) and his entourage. We will return to this scene later.

The multiplicity of epic situations—review, presentation for an outsider, reports, description carefully anchored in the choice of scenes, the manner in which each act begins anew, the introduction of new characters in every act, the way in which the uprising is followed as it spreads (in fact, in the last act a scene even opens one step ahead of the rebels)—all points to the epic basis of the play. It shows clearly that the action and the work are not, as they are in the Drama, identical; the uprising is rather the subject matter of the work. The play's unity is not rooted in the continuity of action but rather in the invisible epic *I* who presents the conditions and events. That is why new figures can keep appearing. The limited number of characters in the Drama serves to guarantee the absoluteness and autonomy of the dramatic whole. Here new figures are regularly brought on stage, and, at the same time, the randomness of their selection, their representativeness, that which points to a collective, is expressed through their appearance.

The epic *I*—paradoxical as it may seem—is a prerequisite for naturalism's "objective" language as it emerges in *The Weavers* and more especially in the original version, *De Waber*. It is precisely in those places where dramatic language foregoes the poetic to approach "reality" that it points to its subjective origins—to its author. The voice of the scientific-minded dramatist is continually audible in this naturalistic dialogue (which anticipates the recordings made later for oral history archives): "This is the way these people talk, I've studied them." In terms of its aesthetics, what is usually considered objective becomes subjective here. A dramatic dialogue is "objective" when it remains within the limits defined by the Drama's absolute form without pointing beyond it to either the empirical world of experience or the empiricist author. In other words, Racine's and Gryphius's alexandrines can be called "objective," as can the blank verse used by Shakespeare and during the German classical period or even the prose in Büchner's *Woyzeck*, in which there is a successful transformation of the dialectal into the poetic.

But the epic form, denied though it may be, has its vengeance at the end of *The Weavers*, just as it did in *Before Sunrise*. Old Hilse condemns the uprising on the basis of faith.

> *Old Hilse*: . . . Why else would I have sat here—why would I have worked this treadle here for forty years until I was almost dead?
> And why would I have sat here and watched him over there living in pride and gluttony, making himself rich on my hunger and misery? Why? Because I had hope. . . . We've been promised. The day of judgement is coming; but we are not the judges: Vengeance is Mine, saith the Lord our God.[1]

He refuses to move from his weaving stool in front of the window.

> Here is where the Heavenly Father has placed me. . . . Here we will
> sit and do what is our duty, though the snow itself catch fire.[2]

There is a volley of fire and Hilse collapses, mortally wounded, the only victim
of the uprising Hauptmann shows on stage. One can see why this ending was
found strange both by the public at contemporary performances for workers and
by bourgeois literary critics. After the opening of the final act, in which Hauptmann's sympathy for the rebels seems to give way to an acceptance of Hilse's
religious convictions, comes this second reversal, which transforms a Drama
about revolution into the almost cynically presented tragedy of a martyr. How
is this to be interpreted? Certainly not from a metaphysical point of view. Here,
too, it seems to be the contradiction between the epic theme and the dramatic
form Hauptmann refused to abandon that is the source of the problem. An under-
stated conclusion would best correspond with the desire to give no further
presentation of the uprising and its suppression. But such a conclusion would be
epic in nature. Because the epic narrator never completely separates his work
from the empirical world, or from himself, he can break it off. After the final
line of the narration comes not nothing but, rather, that no longer narrated "reality," the hypothesis and suggestion of which belong to the formal principles of
the epic. The Drama, however, since it is absolute, is its own reality. It has to
have an end that stands for the end as such and raises no further questions. Instead of breaking off with a look at the suppression of the weaver's revolt,
thereby sticking to the presentation of their collective destiny and at the same
time confirming the epic theme in the formal structure, Hauptmann tried to
satisfy the demands of dramatic form—even though it had from the very beginning been cast into doubt by the subject matter.

Part Two

Transition:
A Theory of Stylistic Change

The crisis experienced by the Drama at the end of the nineteenth century (as the literary form embodying the (1) [always] present, (2) interpersonal, (3) event) arose from a thematic transformation that replaced the members of this triad with their conceptual opposites. For Ibsen, the past dominates instead of the present. The past itself and not a past event is thematized; it is remembered and is still active internally. Thus, the interpersonal is displaced by the intrapersonal. In Chekhov's plays, active life in the present gives way to the reveries of remembrance and utopian thought. Event becomes incidental, and dialogue, the interpersonal form of expression, becomes a vessel for monologic reflection. In the works of Strindberg, the interpersonal is either sublated or seen through the subjective lens of a central *I*. Because of this internalization, (always) present, "real" time loses its position of absolute dominance: past and present flow into each another, the external present calls forth the remembered past. With regard to the interpersonal, the action is reduced to a concatenation of meetings that are simply markers for the actual event: internal transformation. Maeterlinck's *drame statique* eliminates the notion of action. In the face of death, to which this *drame* is wholly dedicated, interpersonal differences—the conflict between one figure and another—also disappear. Death confronts a speechless/blind group of human beings. Finally, Hauptmann's social dramaturgy describes the particularity of interpersonal life in terms of the extrapersonal—political and economic conditions. The uniformity these conditions dictate eliminates the singularity of the (always) present: it is also the past and the future. Action gives way to that conditionality of which humankind is the powerless victim.

Thus, the Drama of the outgoing nineteenth century denies in its content that which, out of obedience to tradition, it still wants to express formally: interpersonal activity. What unites the various works of this period (and can be traced back to the transformation in their thematic) is the subject-object opposition—an opposition that determines their new dimensions. In Ibsen's "analytical drama," present and past, revealer and revealed, confront each another as subject and object. In Strindberg's "station drama," the isolated subject becomes its own object; the humanness of Indra's Daughter is objectified in *A Dream Play*. Maeterlinck's fatalism damns humankind to passive objectivity; the people in Hauptmann's "social Drama" appear in the same objective light. Of course, the thematic of Maeterlinck's and Hauptmann's work can be distinguished from that of Ibsen and Strindberg insofar as it conditions the objectivity of the dramatis personae rather than a subject-object opposition; but the subject, in the guise of an epic *I*, becomes a formal requisite of their presentation.

In this subject-object relationship, the absoluteness of the three fundamental concepts of dramatic form is destroyed and, along with it, that of this form itself. In the Drama, the (1) present is absolute because it has no temporal context: "the drama does not know the concept of time: . . . the unity of time signifies a state of being lifted out of the duration of time."[1] The (2) interpersonal is absolute in the Drama because neither the intra- nor the extra-personal stands next to it. By limiting itself to dialogue, the Drama of the Renaissance elected the sphere of the "inter" as its exclusive space. And the (3) event is absolute in the Drama because it stands above both internal conditioning of the soul and external objective conditions. It alone engenders the dynamics of the work.

When these three factors of dramatic form move into relation as subject or object, they are relativized: Ibsen's present by the past that it must reveal as its object; Strindberg's interpersonal by the subjective perspective in which it appears; Hauptmann's event by the objective conditions that it is supposed to present.

The thematically conditioned subject-object relationship (as a relationship, it is, *eo ipso*, formal in nature) must, of necessity, be anchored in the principle of form governing the work. But the principle of dramatic form clearly represents the negation of any separation between subject and object. According to Hegel's *Aesthetics*, "this objectivity which proceeds from the subject together with this subjectivity which gains portrayal in its objective realization and validity . . . by being *action* provides the form and content of dramatic poetry."[2]

The internal contradiction in the modern Drama, therefore, arises from the fact that a dynamic transformation of subject and object into each other in dramatic form is confronted by a static separation of the two in content. Of course, the Drama in which this contradiction appears must have already resolved it in some provisional fashion to have come into being at all. The contradiction is both overcome and maintained insofar as the thematic subject-object opposition is provided with a foundation within the dramatic form—one that is motivated and, therefore, itself thematic. This subject-object opposition, which is at once formal and contentual, is represented in the fundamentally epic situations (epic poet/object) that, thematically framed, appear as dramatic scenes. Ibsen's problem is that of representing an internally experienced, prior time in a literary form that recognizes internality only in its objectification and time only in its (always) present moment. He solves the problem by inventing situations in which individuals sit in judgment on their own remembered past, which, in this manner, is nudged into the openness of the present. The same problem is posed for Strindberg in the *Ghost Sonata*. It is resolved by the introduction of a figure who knows all about the other characters and, thus, can become their epic narrator within the dramatic fable. Maeterlinck's characters are speechless victims of death. The dramatic scene entitled *Intérieur* shows them as mute figures within the confines of a house. Two characters who watch them from the garden maintain the dialogue—a dialogue that has these mutes as its objects. Hauptmann has a stranger visit the characters he wishes to present. In *The Weavers*, the individual acts represent narrative or revuelike situations. Chekhov eventually solves the problem of representing the impossibility of dialogue within the dialogic form of the Drama by introducing a figure who is hard-of-hearing and by letting the characters speak at cross-purposes.

This rent in the formal principle of the work and the double, formal and contentual, employ of a character or situation—which is bound to harm them—disappear in the dramaturgy of the following decades. But the new forms that mark these years arise out of the formal and thematic conceptions of the transitional period: Ibsen's tribunal on the past; Strindberg's staging of an epic figure; Hauptmann's introduction of a social researcher.

The process, which will be dealt with in detail later, adumbrates a theory of stylistic change that differs substantially from the current explanations about the succession of one style to another. It suggests that a third style, one that is internally contradictory, lies between the two periods and, thus, sets in place the developmental stage, in the tripartite movement of the form-content dialectic. In addition, the transitional period is not simply defined by the fact that, in it, form and content move from an original correspondence (see "The Drama") into opposition with one another (see "The Drama in Crisis"). This sublation up to the next stage of development is, in fact, prepared for in the thematically disguised elements of form already contained within the now problematic old form. And the transformation into a style that is in itself contradictory is realized when a formally operative content is fully precipitated out as form, thereby exploding the old form.

This process, attested to by the resultant twentieth-century dramaturgy, can also be discovered in examples taken from other artistic areas. Within the traditional epic style, a style resting on an opposition between narrator and object, the nineteenth-century psychological novel develops the *monologue intérieur*. This interior monologue no longer presupposes an epic distance, however, since it is fully ensconced in the interiority of the represented characters. As long as the epic style is not abandoned, the *monologue intérieur* must be mediated through the narrator (e.g., the almost stereotypic, "he said to himself," in Stendhal, perhaps the most frequent word group in *Le rouge et le noir*. At the same time, it should be noted that Stendhal's psychological analysis, which takes the psyche as its object, once again legitimates epic distance). As long as it is mediated by the narrator, the interior monologue remains thematic. But the progressive psychologization of the novel in the twentieth century makes the interior monologue more and more essential; the transformation in style (if one omits Dujardain) takes place with Joyce: internal monologue becomes the very principle of form and explodes the traditional epic style. *Ulysses* has no narrator. Just as this stream of consciousness style was prepared for within the traditional narrative, so too Cézanne's painting (to give an extraliterary example), which, finally, maintains the principle of direct observation of nature, already contains the roots of aperspectivism and the synthetic quality of later styles (e.g., the cubists). And Wagner's late romantic music tends toward a thoroughgoing chromaticism and, thus, toward a full acceptance of the twelve-tone scale, thereby preparing for Schönberg's atonality.

Therefore, prior to the collapse of the old style, the new can be discovered lodged in its interior as an antithetical principle.

The three examples—Stendhal, Cézanne, and Wagner—also show that even transitional situations allow for the highest level of completion in a work. But the uniqueness of this reconciliation of contradictory principles—a reconciliation at which these artists succeed—and the immanent dynamics of a contradiction that does not call for reconciliation but, rather, resolution, cannot be overlooked. They explain why the works of these men could not serve as models for later artists or, at least, could become so only insofar as they strove after it in an effort to leave it behind.

Just as "The Drama in Crisis" deduced the transition from the pure style of the Drama to a contradictory dramatic style by examining thematic displacements, the next transformation, which sees little change in thematics, can be conceived of as a process whereby the thematic material was precipitated out as form and exploded the old form. Thus came about those experiments in form that were previously examined only for their own sake and that were, therefore, easily interpreted as childish games, as antibourgeois, or as expressions of personal inability but whose inner necessity becomes clear as soon as they are set within the framework of this change in style.

An example would help here, because it can shed light on the opposition between the thematic and the formal and, at the same time, clarify the process through which form originates. Singing is thematic in a Drama in which a song is sung but formal in the opera. Therefore, the dramatis personae can applaud a chanteuse, whereas the figures in an opera must not show awareness of their singing. (Romantic irony is the term used to describe the fact that the dramatis personae in the comedies of Tieck and others comment on things formal—on their roles, for example.)[3]

Before examining these new forms in which the contradiction between the epic thematic and the dramatic form is resolved, some mention must be made of the trends which, instead of *resolving* the antinomy in the sense of a historical process—that is, instead of letting the form arise from the new content—held fast to dramatic form and tried in various ways to *rescue* it. It must also be noted that these rescue attempts, despite their formalistic-conservative intention, cannot do without new modalities of expression.

Beyond this crisis in the Drama and the attempts at an epic resolution, but fully comprehensible only with them as a background, stands the lyric Drama of the turn of the century, especially the early work of Hofmannsthal. Its indirect connection with the crisis of the Drama is easy to see. The form-content tension of the modern Drama can be traced back to the contradiction between the dialogic unification of subject and object in the form and their confrontation in the content. Epic dramaturgy comes about when the contentual subject-object relation precipitates as form. The lyric Drama escapes this contradiction because the lyric is rooted neither in an actual transformation of each into the other nor in a static separateness from each other with regard to subject and object but, rather, in their essential and original identity. Its central category is mood. But mood does not belong to isolated interiority; at its origin (according to E[mil] Staiger) mood is "precisely not something that exists 'in' us. Rather, through mood, we are emminently 'out there', not confronting objects, but *in* them as they are in us."[4]* And this same identity marks I and you, then and now in the lyric. However, formally, and for the problematic in Ibsen, Strindberg, and Chekhov, this means that the lyric Drama does not distinguish between monologue and dialogue; therefore, the theme of solitude does not call the lyric Drama into question. Dramatic language is tied strictly to an action that unfolds in the uninterrupted present; that is why analysis of the past stands in contradiction to dramatic form. In the lyric, on the other hand, time becomes one, the past is also the present, and speech is not thematic—it needs no motivation and is not subject to interruption by silence. What is lyric is, in itself, speech, and, for this reason, speech and action do not, of necessity, coincide. This is what R[udolf] Kassner suggests when he writes that in Hofmannsthal's early works, "one can, as it were, run one's finger between the language and the action and separate one from the other."[5] Since it is independent of the action, lyric speech is able to cover up the cleft in the events that would otherwise announce the crisis of the Drama.

III. Rescue Attempts

6. Naturalism

The last German Drama that still was Drama was written by Gerhart Hauptmann—one only need think of *Drayman Henschel* (1898), *Rose Bernd* (1903), and *The Rats* (1911). These late successes make possible a naturalism whose conservative tendency in the realm of dramaturgy was already discussed briefly in relation to Strindberg.[1]

Naturalist Drama elected its heroes from the lower strata of society. It found there people whose willpower was unbroken, who could engage their entire being in actions toward which their passion drove them, who were not separated from one another by anything fundamental—neither self-centeredness nor reflection—people who were able to carry the weight of a Drama essentially limited to an (always) present, interpersonal action. Thus, the social difference between the lower and upper classes corresponded to the dramaturgic difference: capacity and incapacity for Drama. Naturalist *parole*, which, with the best of intentions, announced that the Drama was not solely the property of the bourgeoisie, concealed the bitter insight that the bourgeoisie had long since lost possession of it. The question was really one of rescuing the Drama. As one became aware of the crisis in the bourgeois Drama (Hauptmann's *The Coming of Peace* [1890], *Lonely People* [1891], *Michael Kramer* [1900], etc.), one began to flee one's own epoch, not into the past but into the alien present. By climbing down the social ladder, one discovered the archaic in the present; one turned back the hands on the clock of the "objective spirit"—and, as naturalist, became "modern."* The passage of the Drama from the aristocracy to the bourgeoisie in the eighteenth century corresponded to a historical process; the naturalist incorporation of the proletariat on the Drama circa 1900 was, on the other hand, an effort to evade history.

That is the historical dialectic of the naturalist Drama. It has a dramaturgic dialectic as well, however. The social distance that was first made possible by the naturalist Drama was fatal to that same Drama when it became dramaturgic distance. That pity was considered the category central to Hauptmann's writing does not undermine, rather it strengthens the notion that Hauptmann stood before his creatures as their observer and not behind them or in them, because pity presupposes the distance it later overcomes. The true dramatist (and the true spectator), however, does not stand at a distance from the dramatis personae; he is either one with them or not at all present in the work. This identity of author, spectator, and dramatis personae becomes possible because the subjects of the Drama are always projections of the historical subject: they are in full accord with the current state of consciousness. In this sense, every true Drama is a mirror of its epoch; its characters mirror those social classes that, so to speak, embody the avant-garde of the objective spirit. This is the reason there is no true historical Drama. The mythological-historical Drama of the French neoclassical era was that of the aristocracy and the king. The rapprochement between Olympus and the court, which is embodied in Molière's *Amphitryon*, is not simply a piquant bit of eccentricity, it is an expression of the historico-intellectual connection between the age and the *tragédie classique*. And Büchner, despite the greatest care in accurately reproducing parliamentary speeches, did not hesitate to let his Danton parish because of a boredom that, in terms of intellectual history, emerged after Napoleon's fall and became very much his own when he recognized the untimeliness of his revolutionary program. (Stendhal's works are particularly rich in information about the rapport between boredom and the post-Napoleonic situation.) In the naturalist drama, which, thanks to anachronisms in the present, manages to avoid fleeing into history, it is not the turn-of-the-century bourgeoisie nor the class that provisions the Drama with its characters that sees itself reflected. Instead, one group regards the other: the bourgeois author and the bourgeois public observe the agricultural class and the proletariat. This distance leads to some negative consequences in the resultant dramaturgy, however.

As was demonstrated in the analysis of *The Weavers*, the naturalist discourse presupposes an epic *I*. The problem of milieu is closely tied to this fact. The reproduction of milieu cannot simply be explained by way of the naturalist project. It does not just point toward the author's intention, it points to his position as well. The background to peoples' actions, the atmosphere in which they move, these are visible only to the author who stands before them or who visits them as a stranger: the epic narrator. This positioning of the Drama relative to the narrator, which is a prerequisite for the naturalist Drama, is mirrored within it by the relative position the characters assume vis-à-vis their milieu, which seems alien to them. The much-maligned "abstraction" of the *tragédie classique* and the fact that its language is limited to a select vocabulary are fully understandable in terms of the formal principles of the Drama. Abstraction permits events, which here transpire between people and always in the present, to emerge in their greatest purity: the limited vocabulary becomes, as it were, the particular property of the Drama and points not to the empirical (as does naturalist Drama) but beyond it.

Finally, much the same can be said of action. Action in the naturalist Drama usually belongs to the domain of the *fait divers*. The *fait divers* is an event that is interesting enough in itself to be reported, even when alienated from its context. To whom it happens is, therefore, of little consequence; it is essentially anonymous. A newspaper report, for example, "Pauline Piperkarka, servant, twenty years old, living in North Berlin," is sufficient to confirm the validity of the *fait divers*. The movement of the action back into the inner sphere of the subject and the objectification of this interiority in the action (which Hegel demands of dramatic works in general) are precluded by the very nature of the *fait divers*. Therefore, it can never be completely built into the naturalist Drama. It forms a sort of evaporated action within the naturalist text, one into which the characters and their surroundings can never be fully integrated. The dissociation of milieu, character, and action in the naturalist Drama, the alienated condition in which they appear, destroys the possibility of a seamless union of these elements in an absolute and total movement such as that required by the Drama. The movement toward fragmentation that marks almost all of Hauptmann's naturalist works, *Der Rote Hahn* (1901) in particular, is rooted in this problematic, which once again can be solved only within an epic framework: the disparate elements can be united only by an epic *I*.

Thus, naturalist dramaturgy, in which dramatic form attempts to survive its historically conditioned crisis, is, because of the very distance from the bourgeoisie that had at first enabled it to rescue the Drama, constantly in danger of transforming itself into epic.

7. The Conversation Play

A second rescue attempt began on the level of the dialogue. The source of the danger appeared earlier on this level: when the interpersonal relation disappears, dialogue is shredded into monologue; when the past prevails, dialogue is transformed into the necessarily monologic site of memory.

The desire to save the Drama by rescuing dialogue can be traced (especially in theater circles) to the notion that a dramatist is someone who is able to write good dialogue. The preservation of "good dialogue" is achieved by cutting it off from a subjectivity whose historical forms put dialogue into jeopardy. If dialogue in true Drama is the common space in which the interiority of the dramatis personae is objectified, here it is alienated from the subject and appears as an independent entity. Dialogue becomes conversation.

The conversation play dominated European, particularly French and English, dramaturgy from the middle of the nineteenth century. Its identity as the "well-made play" or *pièce bien fait* certified its dramaturgic qualities and thereby hid its basic character, that of an unintended parody of the neoclassical Drama. Its negative aspect—that it did away with the possibility of subjective statement when it was cut off from the subject—turned into something positive when the empty dialogic space was filled with the topical concerns of the day. The conversation play revolves around questions of women's suffrage, free love, divorce law, misalliance, industrialization, and socialism. Thus it acquired the appearance of the modern while actually opposing historical process. As both a modern and an exemplary dramatic model, the conversation play formed the theatrical norm at the beginning of this century. All attempts to produce new statements, new forms, required great effort to separate them from this norm, and they were always criticized on the basis of a comparison with it. Only in Germany was the path through the barricade of the now canonical conversation play less obstructed—because there was no German society and no German conversational style.

Despite this situation, one must not overlook the fact that the conversation play only appeared to be serviceable as a dramatic model. The total transformation of dialogue into conversation leads not only to quantitative but also to dramaturgic retribution. Because the conversation play hovers between people instead of uniting them, it is not binding. Every line of dramatic dialogue is irrevocable and full of consequence. As a causal series, it constitutes its own time and, thus, lifts itself out of the temporal flow. This is what engenders the absoluteness of the Drama. In the case of the conversation play, things are somewhat different. It has no subjective origin and no objective goal; it goes nowhere and is not transformed into action. Therefore, it has no time proper to it alone. Instead, it participates in the movement of "real" time. Because the conversation play has no subjective starting point, it cannot define individuals. Just as the conversation play quotes from the problems of the day, so are the dramatis personae quotations of real social types. But, whereas the typology of, say, the commedia dell'arte is intrinsic to it and refers to an aesthetic reality without pointing beyond its own borders, the typology of the conversation play can be traced back to social typecasting and is, therefore, contrary to the requisite absoluteness of the Drama. Because conversation is not binding, it cannot become action. Action, which is needed for the conversation play to appear "well made," must be borrowed from an external source. Such action is unmotivated. It arrives in the form of unexpected events, which further subvert the absoluteness of the Drama.

The theatricality of the dramaturgy that emerges along with the thematic triviality of the conversation play provides the first real justification for including it in that group of rescue attempts that simply refused to deal directly with the crisis of the Drama. Despite this radical critique of the conversation play, its positive aspects must not be overlooked entirely. They appear at the moment the conversation begins to reflect on itself—when the purely formal becomes thematic.

Hofmannsthal's *The Difficult Man* (1918),* perhaps the most fully realized play in recent German literature, is constructed on the dual foundation of the conversation play and the comedy of character. It escapes emptiness and thematic quotation both because the aristocratic Viennese society it portrays lived mainly in conversation and because this conversation is deepened and transformed by Count Bühl, the title figure, who is the only modern member of that gallery of characters displayed in the major comedies. For him, conversation becomes thematic, and the problematic it generates points out the dubiousness of interpersonal communication and even of language itself.[1]

Everyday French is consolidated in a different manner in Samuel Beckett's *Waiting for Godot* (1952). The otherwise purely formal limitation of the Drama to conversation becomes thematic in this work: nothing but empty conversation remains to confirm the existence of those beings who wait for Godot—this deus not only *absconditus* but also *dubitabilis*. Constantly pressing toward the abyss of silence, retrieved from it over and over again but only with great effort, this hollow conversation still manages to reveal the "anguish of man without God"* in this empty metaphysical space—a space that gives importance to whatever fills it. At this level, of course, dramatic form no longer contains any critical contradictions, and conversation is no longer a means of overcoming such contradictions. Everything lies in ruins—dialogue, form as a whole, human existence. Negativity—meaningless automatic speech and unfulfilled dramatic form—is now the only source of statement. What emerges is an expression of the negative condition of a waiting being—one in need of transcendence but unable to achieve it.

8. The One-Act Play

The fact that, after 1880, dramatists such as Strindberg, Zola, Schnitzler, Maeterlinck, Hofmannsthal, Wedekind, and, later, O'Neill, W. B. Yeats, and others turned to the one-act is not simply a sign that the traditional form of the Drama had become problematic. It also often represents the effort to save "dramatic" style from this crisis by presenting it as a future-oriented style.

The element of tension, of "being ahead of itself" (*Sich-voraus-Seins*, E[mil] Staiger),* is anchored in the interpersonal events of the Drama. It is, finally, the future that is inherent in the dialectic (qua dialectic) between one human being and another. In the Drama, the interpersonal relation is always a unity of opposites that strives toward sublation. Awareness of the necessity of this sublation, the anticipatory thoughts and actions of the dramatis personae as they try to achieve or prevent it, generates a dramatic tension that is quite different from the tension produced by the omens of an approaching catastrophe. The fact that the element of tension is anchored in the dialectic of interpersonal relations explains why the crisis of the Drama also entails a crisis of "dramatic" style in the modern theater. Loneliness and isolation, as they are thematized by Ibsen, Chekhov, and Strindberg, certainly sharpen the opposition between individuals, but, at the same time, they destroy the drive toward the sublation of this opposition. On the other hand, the powerlessness of the individual, which Hauptmann and Zola describe from a social and Maeterlinck from a metaphysical perspective, allows no opposition and leads to the nonconflictual oneness of a fated community. In addition, the process of isolating these figures generally brings with it an "abstraction and intellectualization of their confrontations" in which the sharpened opposition between the isolated individuals is, in a certain sense, always already bridged by means of the objectivity engendered by the intellectualization.[1]

Chekhov's and Hauptmann's Dramas witness to the dwindling tension that results from this process. But the manner in which the one-act is called upon to help provide the theater with an element of tension that is not derived from interpersonal relations is most clearly visible in Strindberg's dramatic oeuvre. The position of the *Eleven One-Act Plays* (1888–92), written between *The Father* (1887) and the station plays *To Damascus I–III* (1897–1904), has already been touched upon.[2] In *The Father*, it becomes clear that subjective dramaturgy no longer corresponds with the traditional form of an unfolding action. Everything is seen from the point of view of the Captain, and his wife's struggle against him is, in the end, also staged by him. The play of oppositions operates within him and can no longer be expressed in terms of an "intrigue." Therefore, in his essay "The One-Act Play" (written in 1889, two years after *The Father*), Strindberg is led to reject intrigue and, with it, the "full-evening play." "A scene, a 'Quart d'heure' seems to be the type of theater piece for people today."[3] This statement presumes not only a quantitative but also a qualitative difference between the one-act and the "full-evening" Drama—in the nature of the unfolding action and (in close relation to it) in the nature of the element of tension.

The modern one-act is not a Drama in miniature but a part of the Drama elevated into a whole. The dramatic scene serves as its model. This means that the one-act, although it does indeed share its starting point, the situation, with the Drama, does not share the latter's action, in which the decisions of the dramatis personae constantly modify the initial situation and move it toward a final point of resolution. Because the one-act no longer draws on interpersonal events for its tension, this tension must already be anchored in the situation. And not simply as a virtual tension that is embodied in each line (this is the manner in which tension is created in the Drama); in the one-act, the situation itself must provide all the necessary information. Therefore, if it is to maintain a semblance of tension, it must elect a borderline situation, a situation verging on catastrophe—catastrophe that is imminent when the curtain goes up and that later becomes ineluctable. Catastrophe is a given, lurking in the future: gone is the tragic personal struggle with a destiny whose objectivity humans could (in Schelling's sense)[4] resist through their subjective freedom. What separates the individual from destruction is empty time, time that can no longer be filled by an action, time that encompasses a pure space stretching out toward catastrophe and within which the individual is condemned to live. Thus, even on the level of form, the one-act proves to be the Drama of the unfree. The period in which it arose was the age of determinism, and this determinism, regardless of stylistic or thematic differences, links the dramatists who seized upon it—both Maeterlinck the symbolist and Strindberg the naturalist.

Maeterlinck's one-acts, his *drames statiques*, have already been considered. Therefore, it will only be necessary to add a comment on this "dramatic" characteristic that is produced by the situation of catastrophe. Nothing would be further from the truth than to conclude from their static condition (which Maeterlinck emphasized in programmatic fashion) and their hidden epic structure that these plays lack the tension that is the hallmark of the Drama as such. The powerlessness of the characters no doubt precludes action or struggle and, thus, interpersonal tension as well, but it does not prevent tension from arising out of the situation into which these individuals are thrust—a tension they must endure while being sacrificed to the situation. Time, stretched taut, time in which nothing more can happen, is filled with growing anxiety and reflection on death. In *The Blind* and *Home*, this tension is no longer marked by the approach of death—it too lies in the past; the timespan is simply that required for death to be discovered. And, as always when it is not filled with action, time is spatialized—like the path to knowledge in *The Blind* and like the path the message takes in *Home*. From the scenic point of view, this becomes palpable [in *The Blind*] as the diminishing distance between the blind and their dead guide (who had, from the beginning, lay in their midst) and [in *Home*] as the line separating the seemingly well protected home (in which the family, free of care, awaits nightfall) from the garden in which two men stand who know about the daughter's suicide but who hesitate to erase this boundary by communicating their knowledge of her death. And in each case, the curtain falls when the path of knowledge or that of the message has, nonetheless, been traveled to its end—when the catastrophe has been experienced and the "pro-ject" (E[mil] Staiger) that created the tension has been overtaken.*

Strindberg's one-act *In the Face of Death* (1892), which carries on the thematic line of *The Father*, is not unlike the *drames statiques* in its basic conception. It can be regarded as a transposition of the latter into the one-act form which, at this point in his development, Strindberg thought "might be the formula for the drama to come."[5] By examining the play in this light, we can see what distinguishes the one-act from the "full-evening play" and what allows it to stand in for the now rather problematic Drama. Mr Durand, "pension manager, formerly an official in the state railroad administration," is a "man in a female hell," as was the Captain in *The Father*. But because he is a widower, he no longer has an antagonist—a sign indicating Strindberg's renunciation of intrigue and, at the same time, the movement of the one-act, which no longer inscribes an event, toward the "analytical technique." The "female hell" is created by Durand's daughters, who oppose him because their mother has raised them to do so. The threat of destruction does not come from them, however, but from outside his family: the pension that he manages is on the verge of bankruptcy. This shift corresponds to a displacement of the interpersonal by the objective, the refounding of dramatic tension, which will now be guaranteed by the situation rather than by a conflict between individuals. To be sure, Strindberg does not make his hero completely helpless. Durand escapes bankruptcy by setting fire to his house and taking poison so that his daughters can live comfortably from his insurance benefits. But the "action" of this one-act is not a series of incidents leading to his decision to kill himself or a portrayal of the psychological development that precedes this decision. Instead it is an exposition of family life undermined by hate and discord—an Ibsenesque analysis of an unhappy marriage, which, in the taut space of approaching catastrophe, achieves "dramatic" efficacy despite the absence of any additional new action.

In some of Strindberg's other one-acts, *Pariah, Playing with Fire*, and *Creditors*, for example (all of which can be termed "analytical dramas" without secondary action in the present), the moment of tension engendered by an impending catastrophe is also absent. It must be admitted that dramatic precipitation in this case originates in the impatience of the reader or spectator, who can no longer bear the hellish atmosphere that has been revealed and who, beginning with the opening exchange, has been thinking ahead to the end—an end that holds out the hope of his deliverance if not that of the figures in the Drama.

At this point, it is necessary to repeat that in Strindberg's work the one-act form was adopted at the moment of crisis. When he realized subjective Drama had surrendered the style of tension at the same time it had given up the direct portrayal of interpersonal events—after a five-year pause—Strindberg turned to the epic formulation found in the station technique.

9. Constraint and Existentialism

The crisis experienced by the Drama in the second half of the nineteenth century can also be traced to the forces that drove people out of interpersonal relations and into isolation. The dramatic style called into question by this isolation survived nonetheless because the isolated individual, whose formal equivalent is silence or the monologue, was forced back into the dialogic of the interpersonal relation by an external agency. This transpired in a situation of constraint, which is the basis for most of the recent Drama that has escaped the movement toward the epic.

The historical origin of this situation can probably be found in bourgeois tragedy. In the preface to *Maria Magdalena* (1844), Hebbel indicates that "the internal element particular to [such tragedy]" is the "harsh closure with which individuals incapable of dialectic face each other in the most confined of spheres."[1] One wonders whether Hebbel was conscious of touching on both the crisis and the salvation of the Drama in this formulation. "Closure" and the incapacity to engage in any (interpersonal) "dialectic" destroyed the possibility of the Drama that had arisen from the decision of individuals to disclose themselves to one another.* It did so at least as long as the "most confined of spheres" did not force open this closure, as long as these isolated individuals, isolated although chained to one another, individuals whose discourse strikes wounds in the closure of the other, were not forced to join in a second dialectic. The constraint that reigns here denies people the space they need to be alone with their monologues or silent and alone with themselves. In a literal sense, the speech of one wounds the other, it breaks through his closure and forces him to reply. Dramatic style, which the impossibility of dialogue threatens to destroy, is rescued at the very moment when, under constraint, monologue itself becomes impossible and, of necessity, turns back into dialogue.

This dialectic between monologue and dialogue is the basis for works such as Strindberg's *Dance of the Dead* (1901) (actually *The Dance of Death*) and Lorca's *The House of Bernarda Alba. A Drama about Women in the Villages of Spain* (1936). The longing for solitude and silence, and their impossibility in a situation of constraint, is expressed clearly by one of Lorca's heroines. Bernarda Alba, whose husband is dead, has transformed her home into a prison for her daughters, a prison of mourning. Early in the play she says that "for the eight years of mourning, not a breath of air will get into this house from the street. We'll act as if we'd sealed up doors and windows with bricks. That's what happened in my father's house—and in my Grandfather's house."[2] The second act shows "a white room in Bernarda's house. . . . Bernarda's daughters are seated on low chairs, sewing." Magdalena notices the absence of Adela, the youngest daughter, and goes to find her. Then:

(Magdalena and Adela enter.)
Magdalena: Didn't you say she was asleep?
Adela: My body aches.
Martirio (*with hidden meaning*): Didn't you sleep well last night?

Adela: Yes.
Martirio: Then?
Adela (loudly): Leave me alone. Awake or asleep, its no affair of
  yours. I'll do whatever I want to with my body.
Martirio: I was just concerned about you!
Adela: Concerned? —curious! Weren't you sewing? Well, continue. I
  wish I were invisible so I could pass through a room without being
  asked where I was going![3]

Earlier Drama has nothing like this. The interpersonal relation and its verbal
expression (dialogue, question and answer) were not painfully problematic.
They were, rather, the self-evident, formal context within which the immediate
theme moved. Here, on the other hand, this formal condition for the Drama itself becomes thematic. The problem that faces the dramatist at this point was
first noted by Rudolf Kassner. In an early essay on Hebbel's characters, he wrote
that "they really resemble people who, after spending a long time alone in solitude and silence, are suddenly expected to speak. In general, speaking is much
easier for the author than for his characters at such moments, therefore, he often
takes over where we would prefer to see them speak."[4] In this statement, Kassner already anticipates the tendency toward the epic in the Drama: the inclusion
of the author, who begins to speak in the guise of the epic *I*. Later, Kassner adds
that "one may say these people are born dialecticians—but they are so only su-
perficially and against their will. First of all and fundamentally, one senses in
all these characters the individual who has long been alone and silent, the individual who, although brought into the play by the author, could also be a spectator."[5] The dramatist's activity is once again the focus here—an activity that first
becomes visible during the Drama's crisis period. It becomes even more visible
in those works whose thematic constraint represents a secondary, formal expe-
dient for enabling the drama. Constraint is justified only when it is an essential
part of the lives of the individuals whose dramatic representation it makes possible. Such is the case in bourgeois tragedy, in Strindberg's marital Drama, and
in Lorca's Drama of social convention. Because this constraint determines the
fate of the dramatis personae, because the characters and their situation are not
separated by a gap, the dramatist remains unseen. The situation is quite different
in the numerous recent theatrical works in which the characters, because of a
dramaturgic act prior to the Drama, are displaced in a situation of constraint that
is in no way characteristic for them but nonetheless makes their entrance into
the Drama possible. Such works are set in a prison, a locked house, a hideout,
or an isolated military post. Reproduction of the particular atmosphere of these
places should not prevent us from recognizing their formal role, however. And,
as in the conversation play, the dramatic style that they make possible has more
appearance than reality. The absoluteness of such accidental situations of constraint is canceled both by the dramatis personae, who point the way out of the

situation (which is external to them) back to their epic origins, and by the dramatist, who is drawn into the work as the subject of this crowding of characters.
The internal dramatic tension is, as it were, purchased at the price of an epic
exterior. What comes of this is Drama in a glass house. The "picture-frame"
stage, which was meant to create a closed sphere for the neoclassical Drama,
one that could reflect a reality limited to interpersonal relations, becomes a wall
fending off the epic aspects of the world outside, becomes a retort: what occurs
within is no longer a reflection, it is a transformation that takes place because
of the dramaturgic "experiment in compression." This dramaturgy is infected by
the artificiality of such constructions; too much is invested in making it formally
possible for its thematic space to remain undamaged. This attempt to rescue dramatic style can be artistically justified only when it can free itself from its artificiality. This is exactly what seems to take place in those dramatic works
produced by existentialism.

Existentialism, as a Weltanschauung and as literature, is an effort, however
problematic, to create a new classicism aimed at preserving naturalism. Limitation to the human was essential for both the neoclassical spirit and the neoclassical style: neoclassical philosophy was humanistic; the notion of freedom
was central to it. Neoclassical style was perfected in those artistic genres whose
formal principles were based completely on the human being: tragedy and
sculpture.

Naturalism is always a late phase in the process of reification. Around 1900,
before they broke with their own formal principles, which date back to the Middle Ages, the novel and painting were naturalistic. But the Drama, when it became naturalistic, began to resemble the novel, and its settings became genre
paintings.

Naturalism's central category is milieu—the quintessence of everything alien
to the individual and to which a hollow subjectivity must finally submit.

Existentialism attempts to return to the neoclassical by cutting through the
controlling power that milieu exercised over the individual. It radicalizes the
alienation. Milieu becomes situation, and, from that moment on, the individual,
no longer bound to milieu, becomes free—but within a situation that is simultaneously his own and alien to him. Free, not merely in the private sense, he
first confirms his freedom by deciding for the situation, by binding himself to
it, in accord with the existential imperative of engagement.

The affinity between existentialism and the neoclassical depends on this
reestablishment of the notion of freedom. It is also the condition that seems to
make the rescue of dramatic style possible. Indeed, existential dramaturgy
stands in close proximity to those efforts that employed the situation of constraint
to save the Drama from contamination by the epic. Owing to a strange agree-
ment between the formal elements of such an effort and the thematic intentions
of the existential dramatist, form, which prior to this had been empty, was able

to make a formal statement and, thereby, to release the dramaturgy of constraint from its artificiality.

This artificiality is rooted in the pretextual, dramaturgic displacement of the characters in a situation of constraint and in the accidental nature of this situation. It is because of its intellectual presuppositions, however, that existentialism demands precisely this displacement and this accidental quality for its thematic — the essential strangeness of situation and the perennial human condition of "having been thrown" — can, from the dramaturgic point of view, only become evident in an action that (according to existentialism) is marked by these general features of human existence. The essential strangeness of every situation must be transformed into the accidental strangeness of the situation represented. Because of this, the existential dramatist does not set people in their "normal" surroundings (as the naturalist set them in their milieu), instead, he removes them to a new context. This displacement, which, as it were, repeats the metaphysical "throw" as an experiment, allows the *existentialia*,* that is, "Dasein's character of Being" (Heidegger), to appear in estranged form as the situationally determined experience of the dramatis personae.

Most of J[ean]-P[aul] Sartre's works follow this basic idea. In his first play, *The Flies* (1943), the action of the classical Electra fable is transformed into an existential experiment. Having grown up far from home, Orestes returns to the place of his birth as a stranger, just as every individual, according to existentialist doctrine, enters (is added to) the world. To cease being a stranger in Argos, Orestes must confirm his a priori freedom — by binding himself, by freely surrendering his freedom. He takes vengeance for Agamemnon's death and rids the city of the flies/furies by becoming a murderer and, as a murderer, by drawing the flies to himself. *Morts sans sepultures* (1946) shows six men from a resistance group in prison; *Dirty Hands* (1948) displaces a young man from the bourgeoisie into the communist party. The most complete balance between dramaturgic and existential displacement, where the profound relationship between the dramaturgy of constraint and existential dramaturgy becomes clear, is, however, to be found in *Huis clos* (1944).

The title (*No Exit*) is already an indication that the play experiments with hermetically sealed space. The scene opens in a "Second Empire style" drawing room in hell. That a profane work could be set in hell and depict it as a drawing room can best be explained in terms of the "inversion method" elucidated by G[ünther] Anders in the work of Aesop, Brecht, and Kafka.[6] Through this secularization, Sartre suggests that life in society is hell, but he inverts the predicate and shows that hell is a "drawing room in Second Empire style."* It is in this drawing room, shortly before the curtain falls, that his hero makes the key statement of the play: "Hell, is other people."[7]* This inversion estranges a now problematic existentiale, being-with-others, which is the basis of social life, and which makes the drawing room possible. But in the "transcendental" situation of hell, it is experienced as a new condition.

Formally speaking, this inversion, too, touches on the crisis of the Drama. When being-with-others becomes problematic as an existentiale, the interpersonal relation, the formal principle of the Drama, is called into question. But inversion is also the means of rescuing the dramatic style. Of course the interpersonal relation remains questionable as thematic material, but, thanks to the constraint imposed by the closed "drawing room," it is formally unproblematic. The essential difference between this work and the rest of the dramaturgy of constraint consists of the fact that, here, hell is not a purely formal structure used to make the Drama possible. On the contrary, what is expressed through the inversion is the hidden nature of that very societal form which would otherwise destroy the possibility of the Drama.

The transposition into a "transcendental" situation signifies more than just a distancing from human existence as such; it allows a backward glance at the particularity of that which is entirely one's own. Thus, *No Exit** continues the tradition of the "analytical drama" but without suffering from the errors found in Ibsen's works. Sitting in judgment on one's own past no longer needs to be motivated by some external event (e.g., the arrival of a family member), because it is already contained in the scene of the action. And the backward glance can hardly be called epic here: the past becomes an eternal present for the dead. In this respect, *No Exit** is linked to another tradition, one that may have been founded by Hofmannsthal's *Death and the Fool*. The retrospection that death makes possible gives adequate expression to the process whereby one's own life becomes an object of examination. Hofmannsthal's text gives shape to the life-denying quality of reflection, the "mind overly awake"[8]: on the threshold of death, the life of reflection becomes the object of reflection—a lyric reflection, to be sure. This motif haunts the literature of the twentieth century in several guises and can be found in boulevard pieces as well as in high art. In the *Inconnu d'Arras* (1935), A[rmand] Salacrou allows a suicide to relive "thirty-five years in a fraction of a second," enacted by the people who had been determining factors in his life. And in Th[eodor] Däubler's expressionist manifesto, *The New Standpoint* (1916), one finds the following lines: "According to a popular saying, when someone is hung, he relives his entire life in the final moment. Now that's expressionism!"

IV. Tentative Solutions

10. *I* Dramaturgy: Expressionism

The first meaningful direction taken by the dramaturgy of the new century and the only one that, up to now, has been embraced by an entire generation, did not itself find an answer to the dramatic crisis out of which it arose; instead it borrowed from that great solitary figure who had distanced himself as far as possible from the Drama during the final years of the previous century. In terms of their form, the plays of German expressionism (ca. 1910–25) are indebted to Strindberg's station technique. What is striking here is that the model could be supplied by the work of an author who, more than anyone before him, made private use of the stage by filling it with the fragments of his own life story. It is not simply that Strindberg, by confining himself to his own *I* (for which he had found an adequate form in the "station drama"), had already broken out of the particular into the general; the element of anonymity, of repeatability, and, in a certain sense, of the formal was already contained in his self-portrait, in the picture of the solitary figure. Important evidence for this is his name in *To Damascus*: The Stranger. Because this name equates Strindberg with "Everyman," it is simultaneously more personal and more impersonal, more unequivocal and more ambiguous than a fictive personal name. This is similar to the dialectics of individuation presented in Th[eodor] W. Adorno's *Minima Moralia*. "For however real [the individual] may be in his relation to others, he is," according to Adorno, "considered absolutely, a mere abstraction."[1] The *I* becomes "ever richer as it increases the freedom with which it unfolds itself and reflects" its relation to the object, "while the restriction and hardening that the *I* claims as its origin, by this very fact, limit, impoverish and reduce it."[2] Despite his isolation as an individual, what continues to define the Stranger in the *Damascus* trilogy is the traumatic residue of his former being-with-others. And Strindberg's final work, *The Great Highway*, shows that limiting the point of view to the subject alone erases rather than creates the possibility of subjective, that is, original, statements.[3]

Expressionism adopted Strindberg's station technique to give dramatic form to the individual, to his journey through an alienated world, rather than to interpersonal actions. The formal structure of the "station drama" has already been discussed at length, along with its epic nature, which mirrors the confrontation between the isolated *I* and a world become strange. What remains to be added is a description of the various modes of separateness and the emptiness of the isolated *I* that are precipitated by the Weltanschauung and style of expressionism.

Strindberg's "Stranger" reappears in these works as *The Son* (Hasenclever), *The Young Man* (Johst), and *The Beggar* (Sorge); his road *To Damascus* becomes that of the *Transfiguration* (Toller), the *Red Street* (Csokor), and the timespan *From Morn to Midnight* (Kaiser). The area of the least difference in these "station dramas" is the individuality of their central figures. These plays are distinguished by the particular sphere through which the formally conceived individual is led: the world of fatherly authority and its irresolute opposite in Hasenclever's *The Son*; the world of war in Toller's *Transfiguration*; the metropolis in Sorge's *Beggar*, in Kaiser's *From Morn to Midnight*, and in Brecht's *Drums in the Night*. Paradoxically, expressionist *I* dramaturgy does not reach its peak in the formation of the individual; but instead, and first of all, in the shocking discovery of the metropolis and its pleasure houses. An essential feature of expressionist art as a whole seems to emerge here. Because its exclusive focus on the subject finally leads to the undermining of that same subject, this art, as the language of extreme subjectivity, loses its ability to say anything essential about the subject. On the other hand, the formal emptiness of the *I* precipitates as the stylistic principle of expressionism—as the "subjective distortion" of the objective. This is the reason German expressionism achieved its best and, probably, its most enduring work in the plastic arts and, especially, in graphics (one need only consider the artists in the Dresden "Brücke" group). This relationship is reflected in the interior of the dramatic work: although the station technique does satisfactorily maintain the isolation of the individual on the level of form, it is not the isolated *I* but the alienated world confronting the individual that is expressed thematically. Only through self-alienation, by becoming congruent with alien objectivity, could the subject manage, nonetheless, to express itself.[4]

Of course, in expressionist dramaturgy, the individual is isolated for various reasons. These works do not limit themselves to autobiographical or historical-critical representations of psycho-social isolation like those found in Hasen-clever's *The Son* or in the plays about homecoming by Toller (*Hinkemann*) and Brecht (*Drums in the Night*). Isolation also appears in programmatic form, such as in Kaiser's call for the "renewal of man." As Kaiser emphasizes at one point, "the most profound truth—is always and only found by the lone individual." His "station dramas" show a lone "renewed" man passing through a generally uncom-prehending world (*From Morn to Midnight*). Ultimately this releasing of a single individual from the interpersonal relation corresponds to the highest aspiration of expressionism: capturing *the* human being in terms of an "intuition of es-sences." Isolation thus becomes a method. In one of the most important of ex-pressionism's theoretical texts, one reads:

> Each person is no longer simply an individual bound by duty, moral-ity, society and family. In this art, each becomes the most elevated and the most deplorable of things: *becomes a human being*. Here is the new and unheard of with respect to other epochs. Here the bour-geois notion of the world ceases at last to be thought. Here there are no longer any contexts that veil the image of the human. No stories of marriage, no tragedies arising out of the collision between convention and the need for freedom, no milieu pieces, no harsh employers or carefree officers, no marionettes who, while dangling from the strings of a psychological Weltanschauung, suffer, laugh and play with the laws, standpoints errors and vices of a man made and man-constituted social existence.[5]

The inevitable abstraction and emptiness of the individual already announced in Strindberg's "station dramas" acquire a theoretical foundation here; expressionism consciously chooses to regard the individual as an abstraction. And from this proud rejection of the interpersonal "connections that veil the image of the human" fol-lows a renunciation of dramatic form—a form, however, that makes itself unavail-able to the modern dramatist, for whom those connections had collapsed.

11. The Political Revue: Piscator

Despite the internal contradictions that it contained of necessity, because it was a "social Drama," Hauptman's *The Weavers*—along with a few other naturalist plays (e.g., Gorky's *The Lower Depths*)—remained for decades at the forefront of that dramaturgy that portrayed social conditions. This occurred because the verdict that the social thematic handed down about dramatic form (a verdict al-ready present in *The Weavers*) was at first enforced on the ephemeral level of *mise en scène* rather than in the realm of play writing per se. This is what hap-pens in Erwin Piscator's work, and his *The Political Theater* (1929)—a book rich in documentary as well as in programmatic information—is worth examining in the context of this investigation. This injection of theatro historical events can be justified both in terms of the impact of Piscator's productions on the dramatists of later years and in terms of the negative origins of his efforts in the dramaturgy of his age. "Perhaps my whole style of directing is a direct result of the total lack of suitable plays. It would certainly not have taken so dominant a form if adequate plays had been on hand when I started."[1]

Piscator himself suggested that naturalism was one of the roots of the "political theater,"[2] and his staging of Gorky's *Lower Depths* (one of his early productions, which arose out of problems similar to those discussed in relation to *Before Sunrise* and *The Weavers*) already contained important elements of the political revue, into which Piscator later dissolved the Drama.

> In this early naturalistic work Gorky had painted a picture of a milieu which was conceived in terms of types, according to the conventions of the day, but which still remained narrowly circumscribed. In 1925 I could no longer think in terms of a small room with ten miserable people in it, but only on the scale of the vast slums of the modern city. The subject of discussion was the slum proletariat as a concept. I had to widen the confines of the play to embrace this concept. . . . It was precisely the two moments in the play which we modified to this end which were the most effective in the theater: the opening scene, the snoring and wheezing of a crowd fills the whole stage, the city awakens, streetcar bells ring, then eventually the ceiling was lowered in and closes the room off from its surroundings, and then comes the tumult, not just a little private fight in the back yard, but a whole quarter rebelling against the police, a rising of the masses. Throughout the play my aim was to translate the spiritual anguish of the individual into general terms wherever possible and to make it typical of the present, to open the confined space (by raising the roof) out into the world."[3]

These changes, no doubt adequate for a social dramaturgy, raise questions about dramatic form itself: they deny its absoluteness. The actual stage setting, which in itself is the world of the Drama, a microcosm that stands for the macrocosm, becomes a segment here. Its presentation arises from the notion of the pars-pro-toto. The relationship of the part to the whole, the exemplary significance of limiting the scene to a room and ten people is clearly expressed in the action of lowering the ceiling at the beginning of the performance. Through this gesture, the dramatic scene is brought into contact with the environment it is meant to evoke, and, at the same time, it is enclosed in a demonstrative act and relativized by an epic *I*.

This is the manner in which Piscator corrects the falsification that the "social Drama" necessarily produced because of the contradiction between an alienated and reified conditionality in its thematic and an interpersonal immediacy in its formal postulate. Through a supplementary turn in his *mise en scène*, Piscator ensured that an adequate form would be given to the historical process of reification and "socialization"—the very process that dramatic transposition into the interpersonal overturned and abolished.[4]

This is clearly the intention of all those scenic innovations that are the source of Piscator's fame.

> Conclusive proof can be based only on scientific analysis of the material. This I can only do, in the language of the stage, if I can get beyond scenes from life, beyond the purely individual aspect of the characters and the fortuitous nature of their fates. And the way to do this is to show the link between the events on stage and the great forces active in history. It is not by chance that factual substance becomes the main thing in each play. It is only from the facts themselves that the constraints and the constant mechanisms of life emerge, giving a deeper meaning to our private fates.[5]*

For Piscator,

> man portrayed on the stage is significant as a social function. It is not his relationship to himself, not his relationship to God, but his relationship to society which is central. Whenever he appears, his class or social statum appears with him. His moral, spiritual or sexual conflicts are conflicts with society. . . . A time in which the relationship of individuals in the community to one another, the revision of human values, the realignment of social relationships is the order of the day cannot fail to see mankind in terms of society and the social problems of the times, i.e., as a political being. . . . The excessive stress on the political angle—and it is not *our* work, but the disharmony in current social conditions which makes every sign of life political—may in a sense lead to a distorted view of human ideals, but the distorted view at least has the advantage of corresponding to reality.[6]
> What are the forces of destiny in our own epoch? . . . Economics and politics are our fate, and the result of both is society, the social fabric. . . . Therefore, when I designate the elevation of private scenes to the plane of the historical the basic intent of all stage actions, that can only mean elevation into the political, economic and social. Through them we put the stage in touch with our lives.[7]

The basic formula for Piscator's efforts, the elevation of the scenic to the plane of the historical (formally speaking, a relativizing of the immediacy of the setting by nonactualized objectivity) destroys the absoluteness of the dramatic form and makes way for the rise of epic theater. The use of motion pictures was one means of showing "how human/superhuman factors interact with classes or individuals,"[8] a means that, furthermore, was one of Piscator's clearest and most significant epic gestures.

The development of the motion picture between the end of the century and the 1920s is marked by three discoveries: (1) the mobility of the camera—that is, the shift of focal length, (2) the close-up, and (3) the montage—the composition of an image. With these innovations, film (as B[ela] Baláz's seminal text, *The Visible Man* [1924], has shown) came into possession of means of expression that are particularly its own, through which it finally achieved its position as an autonomous art form. Its discovery, around 1900, was a purely technical achievement: film first served as a technique for bringing the theater to the screen. As a mechanical reproduction of a theatrical production, it could appropriately be called dramatic. But with the artistic discoveries just mentioned (which bring the camera into the picture as a productive force, make modifications of the relationship between camera and object a fruitful means of shaping the image, and allow the sequence of images to be controlled not only by real events but also by the principles of composition used by the director in his montage), the motion picture ceases to be filmed theater and becomes an independent pictorial narrative. It is no longer a technical repetition of the Drama, it is an autonomous, epic art form.

The epic nature of the motion picture, which is grounded in the opposing spaces of the camera and its object, in the subjectively codetermined representation of objectivity as objectivity, allowed Piscator to add to the stage action those things that escaped dramatic actualization—the alienated reification of "the social, the political and the economic." This epic quality allowed him to elevate "the scenic to the plane of the historical."

This is the manner in which Piscator used film in staging such works as Toller's *Hoppla, Such is Life!* (1927). Here as well, it was crucial "to derive the fate of the individual from general historical factors, to establish a dramatic connection between Thomas's fate and the war and revolution of 1918." The central idea of the play was the

> impact of today's world on a man who has spent eight years in isolation. Nine years have to be shown with all their terror, stupidity and triviality. Some conception of the enormities of the period has to be given. The impact will not register with its full force unless the audience sees the yawning chasm. No medium other than film is in a position to let eight interminable years roll by in the course of ten minutes.
>
> For this "film interlude" alone we worked out a script which incorporated four hundred separate items of information about politics, the arts, society, sport, fashion, etc. . . . . A small army [was] constantly on the search for authentic footage of the last ten years.[9]

It is not just the inherent epic nature of film that transforms sociopolitical Drama into epic theater when motion pictures are used in a production. The juxtaposition of stage and screen events also has an epic (relativizing) effect. The action on stage ceases to be the sole foundation for the totality of the work. This totality no longer arises dialectically from interpersonal events. Instead, it is a result of the montage of dramatic scenes, film reports, choruses, projections of calendars, pointed allusions, etcetera. The fact that the various parts have become internally relative to one another is emphasized spatially by the various forms of simultaneous setting that Piscator employed. Even time, in the revue mounted in this manner, is no longer that absolute sequence of events in the present constituted by the Drama. Movies leave past events in the past and represent them documentarily. They can also anticipate future events in the stage action and dissolve the essentially dramatic tension about what will happen in the end by means of epic juxtaposition. In A[lexei] Tolstoy's play *Rasputin*, film permitted a "*confrontation (for the public)*" between the Tzar's family and its fate by showing its execution before the fact on the screen.[10] And last, the choruses and cries that are directed at the public partake of the flow of real time. Behind all these elements of the revue, however, stands the extravagant, larger-than-life epic *I* who brings them together and disseminates them to the public with the gesture of a political orator: Erwin Piscator in persona. That he saw and presented himself in this light is revealed by a now famous setting:[11] on the giant screen of a three-story stage one sees his monumental profile.

12. Epic Theater: Brecht

Bert Brecht, like Piscator, is a descendant of naturalism. His efforts also begin at that point where the contradiction between social thematic and dramatic form becomes visible: in the naturalist "social Drama." It was not naturalism itself but its internal adversary (an adversary that could only appear in thematic disguise while under the dominion of the Drama's rules of form) that was taken up by Piscator and Brecht and led to a breakthrough at the expense of dramatic form. But whereas Piscator, the director, lifted the revue element out of the antithetical structure of the "social Drama" and transformed it into a new principle of form, Brecht, the dramatist, looked deeper. For him it was a question of enthroning the scientific principle, which, although it belongs essentially to naturalism (as Zola's novels prove), can come into its own only by accident in naturalistic Drama — as a dramatis persona, for example (Loth in *Before Sunrise*). Where Hauptmann transforms the Silesian "coal farmers" into objects scrutinized by a stranger who happens to be a sociologist, Brecht shifts this objectivity from thematic contingency into the institutional stability of form. In his "Short Organum for the Theater," he insists that the scientific eye, to which nature was forced to submit, should turn its regard toward those people who subdued nature and whose lives are now determined by its exploitation. The theater should portray the interpersonal relationships that belong to the age in which nature has been mastered, or, more precisely, it should show the "division" between people created by this "gigantic joint undertaking."[1] And Brecht is aware that the necessary condition for this portrayal is a renunciation of dramatic form. The increasingly problematic nature of interpersonal relationships calls the Drama itself into question, since dramatic form asserts that these relationships are unproblematic. This explains Brecht's attempt to oppose the Aristotelian theory and practice with a non-Aristotelian epic dramaturgy.

His Notes to the opera *Rise and Fall of the City of Mahagonny*, published in 1931, lists the following shifts in emphasis from the dramatic to the epic theater.[2]

Dramatic Theater	Epic Theater
The stage "embodies" an event	narrates the event
involves the spectator in an action and	turns the spectator into an observer but
exhausts his capacity for action	arouses his capacity for action
engenders feelings in him	forces him to make decisions
allows him experiences	grants him knowledge
the spectator is transplanted into an action	confronts an action
it operates through suggestion	it operates through argument
sentiments are preserved	brought to the point of recognition
the human being is presumed known	the human being is the object of investigation
he is unalterable	he is alterable and able to change
tension focuses on the conclusion	the tension of process
each scene generates the next	each scene exists for itself
linear development	curves
natura non facit saltus	*facit saltus*
the world as it is	the world as it becomes
what man ought to do	what he must do
his instincts	his reasons for action
thought determines being	social being determines thought

What these changes have in common is that they replace the essentially dramatic transformation of subject and object into one another with an epic confrontation. Thus, in art, scientific objectivity is transformed into epic objectivity and pervades all levels of the stage play—its structure, its language, and its *mise en scène* as well.

The events unfolding on stage no longer completely fill out the performance the way dramatic events had previously. This earlier dramatic practice led to the elimination of the fact of the performance (noted historically in the disappearance of the prologue during the Renaissance). The flow of events is now the object of a stage narrative—the stage is to these events what the narrator is to the object of his narration. It is only the confrontation of the two that produces the totality of the work. Likewise, the spectator is not excluded from the play; neither is he pulled into the play by its suggestive power (caught in its illusion) in such a way that he ceases to be a spectator. Instead, as spectator, he is confronted by the events, which are proposed as an object for his consideration. Because the action does not, by itself, complete and dominate the work, it can no longer transform the time of the performance into an absolute unfolding of time in the present. The present of the performance is, as it were, broader than that of the action; therefore, rather than focusing exclusively on a conclusion that comes of its own course, the performance grants recourse to the past and acknowledges the present course of events as well. The dramatic concern with ends is replaced by an epic freedom to pause and reflect. Since the active individual has now become the object of the theatrical performance, the performance itself can go beyond this individual and ask questions about the causal grounds for his actions. According to Hegel,[3] the Drama shows only that which the hero's subjectivity objectifies in action and that which this action retains of the objective world and transfers into subjectivity. In epic theater, on the other hand, and in line with its scientific-sociological intention, there is a process of reflection on the social "base" of actions and their reified alienation.

As author and director, Brecht produced an almost endless wealth of dramaturgic and scenic ideas in order to transform this theory into practice. These ideas, and those he borrowed, served to isolate and alienate the traditional elements of the Drama and its staging, both of which were familiar to the public. This isolation and alienation from the total movement that typifies the Drama transformed them into scenic-epic elements—that is, into objects on display. Thus, Brecht named them "estrangement effects." Of the profusion of such effects realized or suggested in his works, in the Notes and in his "Short Organum," only a few will be mentioned here.

The play in its totality can be estranged through the use of a prologue, a curtain-raiser, or through the projection of captions. Since it is expressly presented, the play no longer possesses the absoluteness of the Drama; it now refers to the newly uncovered fact of "representation"—becomes the object of this representation. The individual dramatis personae can estrange themselves by introducing themselves or by speaking of themselves in the third person. This is what takes place when Pelagea Vlassova speaks at the beginning of Brecht's adaptation of Gorky's *The Mother*.

> It's such a shame to pour out soup like this for my son. Yet I can't put more fat in. Not even half a spoonful. Only last week they took a ko-pek an hour out of his wages and there's nothing I can do to make up for it. . . . What am I to do—I, Pelagea Vlassova, forty-two years old, the widow of a worker and the mother of a worker?[4]

The roles in a play are further estranged by the actor, who, in the epic theater, is not allowed to submerge himself entirely in the character. "He has just to show the character, or rather has to do more than just get into it; this does not mean that if he is playing a passionate part he must himself remain cold. It is only that his feelings must not at bottom be those of the character, so that the audience's [feelings] may not at bottom be those of the character either.[5] A role can also be estranged by redepicting it in the setting. Or through "subjective descriptions of morals":

> Now let's drink another
> Then we still won't head for home
> Then we'll drink another
> Then we'll take a little break.

Brecht remarks that "the people who sing this are subjective moralists. They are describing themselves."[6] The stage, which no longer signifies the world but only depicts it, loses its absoluteness and, at the same time, loses its apron, which had helped create the illusion that the stage generated its own light. The stage is lit by lamps hung among the spectators—as a clear sign that something is on display for them. The decors are estranged. They no longer give the impression of real places. As an independent element of the epic theater, they "quoted, nar-rated, anticipated and reminded."[7] In addition to indicating the place of action, the stage can also have a screen for projections: texts and documentary pictures can be used (as Piscator did) to show the context in which events take place. The unfolding action, which no longer has the linear resoluteness and necessity of the Drama about it, can be estranged by the projection of textual commentary, by choruses, songs, or even by the cries of "news vendors" in the house. They interrupt the action and comment on it.

> As we cannot invite the audience to fling itself into the story as if it were a river and let itself be carried vaguely hither and thither, the in-dividual episodes have to be knotted together in such a way that the knots are easily noticed. The episodes must not succeed one another

indistinguishably but must give us a chance to interpose our judgment. (If it were above all the obscurity of the original interrelations that interested us, then just this circumstance would have to be sufficiently estranged.)[8]

And to further estrange the spectator, Brecht (following the example of the futurists) suggested that they smoke while watching the play.

Through these estrangement techniques, the subject-object opposition that is at the origin of epic theater (the self-alienation of the individual, whose own social being has become reified) is precipitated formally on all levels of the work and, thus, becomes its general formal principle. Dramatic form rests on the interpersonal relation; the thematic of the Drama is constituted by the conflicts generated by this relation. Here, on the other hand, the interpersonal relation becomes entirely thematic and is removed from the certainty of form to the uncertainty of content. And the new formal principle consists of a pointed distance between the individual and what has become questionable; the epic subject-object opposition appears in a scientific-pedagogical modality in Brecht's epic theater. In the "Short Organum," he designates "the exposition of the story and its communication by suitable means of alienation" as "the main business of the theater."[9]

13. Montage: Bruckner

To give scenic expression to the separation marking the lives of the people of his era, Strindberg set the facade of a house on stage. But its role was of a subordinate and even antithetical nature in the formal whole of *The Ghost Sonata*—a role that revealed only the general contradiction between the theme of isolation and the dramatic form that pervades this work. The apartment house, with its numerous places of action, remained in the background. The square in front of the house ensured the unity of place. And in this open scenic space, it is the mediation of Hummel, the company director, that allows the motif embodied by the closed house to achieve dramatic form. He tells the Student, a "stranger"[1] who happens to be passing by, about the occupants of the house. Thus, the epic process—narration itself—appeared in the guise of a dramatic fable.

On the other hand, two dramatists of the 1920s, Georg Kaiser in *Side by Side* (1923) and Ferdinand Bruckner in *The Criminals* (1929), tried to provide an unmediated view of the epic quality inherent in life when it is lived "next to" rather than "with" others. They attempted to go beyond the Drama to give this epic situation adequate form. Yet, there is a particular affinity between *The Criminals* and *The Ghost Sonata*.

Bruckner, too, set a three-story house on stage, but his three stories filled the entire stage. When the curtain went up, it was not a square in front of the house that came into view, as in *The Ghost Sonata*, but seven separate rooms inside the house. This also made it possible to forgo the use of figures whose task it was to mediate between the epic theme and dramatic form. Hummel was, as it were, moved into the background and reabsorbed in the formal subjectivity of the work. The Student, on the other hand, was shifted forward, into the house. Their juxtaposition, which, in *The Ghost Sonata*, creates a motivated narrative situation that is inscribed in the dramatic form, was recast by Bruckner as a confrontation between the invisible epic *I* and the spectator—a confrontation which is itself the new principle underlying form.

At this point, the manner in which the action unfolds changes too. Since *The Ghost Sonata* held fast to dramatic form, it could not portray the side-by-side existence of individuals as a synchronous unfolding of separate actions. Only the first act could present them in their separateness, since in that act these individuals were not carriers but merely objects of the dialogue. The second act, however, assembled them at the "ghost supper" and combined their fates into a single dramatic action. In *The Criminals*, Bruckner handles the problem differently. In this work, the simultaneous setting corresponds to the temporal dimension in which five individual actions run parallel to one another. Of course, these actions are connected, but not in the manner dramatic form requires. They are not provided with concrete links to a single situation; instead, their connection stems from the fact that they are individually tied to the same theme, to the possible congruity or incongruity that may exist between legal decisions and justice. *The Criminals* is not just a play about how people exist next to but separate from one another, it is also about the problem of justice. The unity of these two themes becomes clear during a conversation in the second act of Bruckner's work, in which two judges argue about the nature of justice.

> *Older Judge*: The community of man is predicated on a shared notion of the law.
> *Younger Judge*: And I have only seen real demonstrations of community at those moments when this shared notion of the law has been overthrown, at those moments when one talks about criminals. The negative form is that of dull, egocentric, side by side existence, of watching, of non-participation. Those are the only real crimes, since they have their origin in a complacency of the heart, an inertia of the spirit—thus a total denial of the principle of life and the idea of a community. But these crimes are left unpunished. The other, opposite sort of actions indicate a will to life, and that alone is sufficient to deem them positive, but in every case in which a verdict is rendered, they are punished as crimes.[2]

The reversal of the relationship between communication and isolation proposed here with regard to justice and injustice, rule and exception, certainty and doubt, is central to the formal concept of the play. The interpersonal relation is the unproblematic/formal framework for the Drama. By answering the call of duty, the tragic hero separates himself from this framework and makes himself guilty of isolation, as does the comic character when at the mercy of an idée fixe. Thus, the problematic of an actualized/thematic isolation remains within the certainty of the interpersonal while emerging at the two extremes of the Drama, tragedy and comedy. Not so in Bruckner's play. Its unproblematic framework is life disjoined—isolation. Therefore, an epic presentation, a structure in which an isolated being is placed in relation to the epic *I*, replaces dramatic form and the absoluteness of interpersonal events. When this happens, communication becomes thematic—becomes an exception and is perverted to the criminal within the space of "egocentric, side by side existence." This thematic reintroduction of the interpersonal in no way allows the epic work to fold itself back into the dramatic, however. Instead, the dubious/objective nature of the interpersonal calls for further representation. Within the epic form, which already contains a subject-object relationship, the interpersonal must appear as the object in a second thematic relation. The second and central act satisfies this exigency: the incidents of the first act reappear, but are objectified thematically as the focus of courtroom proceedings.

This thematic consolidation corresponds to that which takes place formally. In a loose combination of juxtaposed and successive steps, the first act marks the descent into crime of a few inhabitants of the tenement: a poor, old woman who sells the jewelry she has been saving for her brother-in-law in order to raise her children; a young girl who wants to kill herself and her newborn baby, but hesitates in the face of death, saves herself, and thus becomes a child murderer; a cook who kills her rival and shifts the suspicion onto her sweetheart to take vengeance on him too; a young man who gives testimony in favor of a blackmailer because he wants to hide his homosexuality; and a young employee who dips into the till so he can travel abroad with the mother of a friend. All of this is depicted in the first act, but not dramatically—not by meshing the individual moments. Instead, a few pregnant scenes, presented in loose succession, point the way to the past and the future. Actually they sketch rather than represent the actual events. The scenes do not engender one another in closed functionality as in the Drama; they are the oeuvre of the epic *I*, who shifts his spotlight from one place in the tenement to another. The spectator catches fragments of dialogue. When he has grasped their significance and can imagine the results, the light moves on and illuminates another scene. Everything is thus relativized by the epic technique and integrated into a narrative act. The individual scene does not dominate as it does in the Drama; the spotlight can leave it at any moment, can thrust it back into the dark. This shows that reality has neither achieved dramatic openness on its own nor moved continually within such openness. Rather, reality must first be disclosed through an epic process. Of course, this process cannot function without dialogue because it does not allow its *I* to speak as narrator, but it does make it possible for the dialogue to disavow itself. Because the dialogue no longer has to take responsibility for the forward movement of the work (the epic *I* guarantees this movement), it can unravel into Chekhovian monologue or even revert to silence and thereby renounce dialogue as such.

The diversity of the first act contrasts with the unity of the second. Even though simultaneous settings are used again and three floors of a criminal court appear in place of those of the tenement, the relationship between the individual spaces and actions is now totally different. Their simultaneousness is augmented by a unity that is revealed in the courtroom proceedings. They no longer show different aspects of life in a metropolis but, instead, the mechanical uniformity of legal judgments. A formal modification marks this shift. The scene changes no longer depend on the narrator's freedom to turn first to one group of figures and then to another. What is essential now is that the fragments of the various proceedings blend to form a unified picture of the court of law. This is achieved by using the domino principle of fictive sameness to blur the transitions. One trial breaks off at the point where a judge says, "The evidence is clear," the area is darkened, another courtroom is lit, and the spectator enters a new trial at the point where a new judge utters the same words.[3] Thereafter, other expressions are used in the same manner: "I ask the witness"[4]; "Do you know the accused?"[5]; "The prosecutor has the floor"[6]; "The idea of punishment would lose all meaning"[7]; "What is the nature of justice?"[8]; and "In the name of the people"[9]. The individual scene transcends its dramatic exclusiveness in each of these phrases. Each scene quotes from the world of real courts of law and, through the quotation, slips into another scene. There is no organic bond between two successive scenes. Continuity is simulated by their articulation with regard to a third term with which they are associated: the court of law. They form a montage. The formal-historical significance of this technique can only be alluded to, because it belongs to the pathology of the epic and painting and not to that of the theatrical work. That the tendency toward the epic in the dramaturgy of the twentieth century did not secure the position of the epic, that, even in the interior of the epic, antithetical forces accumulated, becomes evident quite by chance in the example of the *monologue intérieur* discussed earlier.[10] Not only interiorization and its methodological result, psychologization, but also the alienation of the external world and its corollary, phenomenology, stand in opposition to the traditional role of the epic narrator.[11] In addition, montage is the epic art form that disavows the narrator. While narration perpetuates the narrative act—does not break the link with its subjective origin, the narrator—montage freezes at the moment of its production and, like the Drama, fosters the impression that it in itself embodies something whole.* It points to the narrator only as to a brand name—montage is mass-produced epic.

14. Enacting the Impossibility of the Drama: Pirandello

*Six Characters in Search of an Author** has for decades been considered by many to be the quintessence of the modern Drama. However, its historical role hardly corresponds to the occasion that, according to Pirandello's preface, inspired the play: a breakdown in the workings of his imagination. The question is, why are the six characters "in search of an author"; why did not Pirandello become this author? In response, the dramatist explains that fantasy once brought six characters into his house. But he rejected them, because he saw no "higher meaning" in their fate that could justify giving them form. Only their stubborn desire for life allowed Pirandello to discover this "higher meaning," but it was no longer what he had expected. Instead of the Drama of their past, he composed the Drama of their new adventures—their search for a different author. There is no reason to cast critical doubt on this statement; nor is the critic prevented from placing another next to it, one that can be extracted from the work itself, one that eliminates mere accident as its reason for coming into being and points out the historical significance of this origin. Soon after the entrance of the six characters—another play is being rehearsed on stage—their spokesman mentions the dramatist's rejection and enlarges in the following manner on the explanation given in the preface: "the author who created us alive no longer wished, *or was no longer able*, materially to put us into a work of art."[1]* The notion that it was less a question of will than of ability or, objectively stated, of possibility is confirmed frequently throughout the rest of the play. The attempt made by the six characters to stage their Drama with the help of the rehearsing troupe not only makes it possible to recognize the piece that Pirandello allegedly refused to write but also grants insight into the reasons why that play was doomed to failure from the start.

It is an analytical Drama in the vein of Ibsen's late works or Pirandello's *Henry IV* (which was written at about the same time as *Six Characters*). The first act unfolds at the home of the procuress, Madame Pace, where a visitor discovers that the girl offered him is his step-daughter. This act closes with the shrill cry of his former wife, the girl's mother, who has suddenly appeared. The place of action for the second act is the garden of the Father's house. He takes back his ex-wife and her three children despite his son's objections. Each of them is hostile toward the others: The Son toward the Mother, because she left the Father; the Step-Daughter toward her step-father, because of his visit to Madame Pace's; the Father toward the Step-Daughter, because she judges him solely on the basis of this one faux pas; the Son toward his half-sister, because she is the child of a stranger. In an Ibsenesque analysis, the parent's past is slowly revealed and the error in the Father's well-intended but destructive principles is discovered. "All my life I have had these confounded aspirations towards a certain moral sanity,"[2]* is his explanation for the fact that he married a woman because of her humble origins, without loving her; that he took her son from her to give him to a wet nurse in the country. When the Mother receives sympathy and understanding from her husband's secretary, the Father believes he must forgo his claim to her, so he lets them establish a new family. Even the benevolent interest that he shows them afterward proves to be pernicious: out of jealousy, the secretary goes abroad with his wife and children, and they are forced to return home in poverty when he dies. The Mother sews for Madame Pace, her daughter delivers the finished work. The play ends with an unmotivated catastrophe, as do many "analytical dramas": one child drowns in a well and the other shoots himself with a pistol.

The project of completing this play according to the rules of classical dramaturgy would not only have required Ibsen's mastery but his blind violence as well. Pirandello clearly saw the manner in which the material and its intellectual postulates would resist dramatic form, however. Therefore, he did without it, and instead of overcoming the resistance, he firmly confined it to the thematic. Thus arises a work that replaces the one originally planned—a work that deals with the impossibility of the latter.

The conversations between the six characters and the manager of the troupe not only present a sketch of the original play but also give expression to the forces that, ever since Ibsen and Strindberg, have called the Drama into question. The Mother and Son are reminiscent of Ibsen's characters[3]; but because they are not subdued by the dramatist, they can reveal how much they hate dialogic-scenic openness.

> *The Mother*: I beg you, sir, to prevent this man from carrying out his
> plan which is loathsome to me.[4]
> My God! Why are you so cruel? Isn't it enough for one person to support all this torment? Must you than insist on others seeing it also?[5]
> *The Son*: I had rather not say what I feel and think about it. I
> shouldn't even care to confess to myself. No action can therefore be
> hoped for from me in this affair.[6]
> Have you no decency, that you insist on showing everyone our
> shame? I won't do it! I won't! And I stand for the will of our author
> in this. He didn't want to put us on the stage, after all.[7]

Even the fact that the Son's attitude makes the unity of place impossible is discussed—it would require him to interact precisely with those others from whom he wishes to withdraw:

> *The Manager*: Are we going to begin this second act or not?
> *The Step-Daughter*: I'm not going to talk any more now. But I must
> tell you this: you can't have the whole action take place in the garden, as you suggest. It isn't possible.
> *The Manager*: Why not?

The Step-Daughter: Because he (*indicates the Son again*) is always shut up alone in his room.[8]

In other scenes, naturalism prevails in the daughter's protests. The idea of the theater as an imitation of reality is so strong here that it is doomed to failure—a failure produced by the irreconcilable difference between the real scene and the theatrical scenery, between the character and the actor.[9] At the same time, the Step-Daughter represents the Strindbergian *I* that demands sole rule of the stage. The criticism she receives from the Manager because of this can be read as a critique of subjective dramaturgy in general.

The Step-Daughter: . . . but I want to act my part, *my part*!
The Manager: (*annoyed, shaking his shoulders*) Ah! Just *your* part! But, if you will pardon me, there are other parts than yours: His (*indicating the Father*) and hers! (*indicating the Mother*) On the stage you can't have a character becoming too prominent and over- shadowing all the others. The thing is to pack them all into a neat little framework and then act what is actable. I am aware of the fact that everyone has his own interior life which he wants very much to put forward. But the difficulty lies in this fact: to set out just so much as is necessary for the stage, taking the other characters into consideration, and at the same time hint at the unrevealed interior life of each. I am willing to admit . . . that . . . it would be a fine idea if each character could tell the public all his troubles in a nice monologue or a regular one hour lecture.[10]

But it is only in the role of the Father that Pirandello's deepest concerns are expressed. That they involve the breakup of the Drama remains, of course, unsaid—either because the Father has hopes of actually creating a Drama or be- cause Pirandello did not want to imply that his ideas were valid only for the Drama. Nevertheless, the existential presuppositions for the Drama have seldom been called into question so sharply as by the subjectivity of Pirandello's philoso- phy of life. It is on this before all else that the Drama of the six characters founders, and it also explains their forever unsuccessful search for an author.

The Father: But don't you see that the whole trouble lies here. In words, words. Each one of us has within him a whole world of things, each man of us his own special world. And how can we ever come to an understanding if I put in the words I utter the sense and value of things as I see them; while you who listen must inevitably translate them according to the conception of things each one of you has within himself. We think we understand each other, but we never really do.[11]
For the drama lies all in this—in the conscience that I have, that each one of us has. We believe this conscience to be a single thing,

but it is manysided. There is one for this person, and another for that. Diverse consciences. So we have this illusion of being one person for all, of having a personality that is unique in all our acts. But it isn't true. We perceive this when, tragically perhaps, in something we do, we are as it were, suspended, caught up in the air on a kind of hook. Then we perceive that all of us was not in that act, and that it would be an atrocious injustice to judge us by that action alone, as if all our existence were summed up in that one deed.[12]

If the first of these quotations denies the possibility of verbal understanding, the second takes aim at action as a valid objectification of the subject. Contrary to the creed of dramatic form, which holds that dialogue and action are, in their finality, an adequate expression of being, Pirandello sees in them an illicit and injurious limitation on the endless multiplicity of internal life.

As a critique of the Drama, *Six Characters in Search of an Author* is an epic rather than a dramatic work. As in all "epic dramaturgy," that which had constituted the form of the Drama is thematic here. The fact that this theme is not dealt with as the general problem of the interpersonal (as in Giraudoux's *Sodome et Gomorrhe*) but, rather, in terms of the questionable nature of the Drama, as a search for an author and an effort at dramatic realization, explains the special position of this work in modern dramaturgy. It becomes almost a self-representation of the history of the Drama. At the same time, it represents a further, intermediate step in the development of the epic. The subject-object opposition is still masked, but this mask is no longer at one with the real action (as it still is in Strindberg's *Ghost Sonata* and Hauptmann's *Before Sunrise*).[13] The thematic operates on two different levels: the dramatic (the past of the six characters), which is no longer able to generate a form, and a second level that answers for the form and is epic in its relation to the first. This second level corresponds to the appearance of the six characters at the rehearsal and the attempt to embody their Drama. They narrate and perform their fate themselves with the Manager and his troupe as their public. The breakup of the dramatic nexus is not yet complete, however, because the epic action that frames the first (dramatic) level makes use of dramatic form and, thus, raises no questions about interpersonal actuality—the very thing that, in the real movement of the play, cannot be relied on. Only when the narrative situation is no longer thematic and no longer dialogic/scenic can the idea of the epic theater be fully realized. Otherwise it will always be open to the seduction of a pseudo-dramatic conclusion. In *Six Characters*, the two thematic levels, whose separation constitutes the formal principle of the work, become one in the end: a shot kills the Boy both in the past narrated by the six characters and in the present on stage while the actors rehearse. And the curtain, which, following the dictates of the epic theater,[14] was already up at the beginning in order to mix the reality of the rehearsal with that of the spectators, falls, nonetheless, in the end.

15. *Monologue Intérieur*: O'Neill

Dramatis personae have always been able to avail themselves of an occasional aside. But such passing suspension of dialogue does not refute the assertion that dramatic form has dialoguing as its principle; nor is it the famous exception that proves the rule (this expression is meaningless). Instead, it is indirect proof of the strength of the dialogic stream, which survives such interruptions as if it were beyond dialogue. This is possible, however, only because the aside, as it is known in genuine Drama, has no tendency to destroy dialogue; here too, G[eorg] Lukács's previously cited comment about the monologue holds true.[1] The content of the *à part* is not essentially different from that of dialogue.* It does not come from a deeper stratum of the subject and is not in some sense the inner truth that shows dialogue to be the lie of the external. It is not by accident that comedy is the special realm of the *à part*: in comedy the possibility of communication is compromised least of all, and there is no need for an inner, psychic reality. But the momentary destruction of this secure dialogic realm is what is most comic. Thus the misunderstanding and confusion that make up the whole of such works as Molière's farce *Sganarelle; ou, Le cocu imaginaire*. In it the *à part* reveals its main function: to give pointed emphasis to the misunderstanding and confusion. Furthermore, it is no accident that the great dramatists of the past did not use the *à part* in the most deeply problematic encounters of their plays, whereas, in like situations, such means would force themselves upon today's authors. One need only reread Racine's dialogue between Phaedra and Hippolytus[2] or Schiller's between Mary and Elizabeth[3] to see the difference. It is precisely because the dialogic structure is being attacked at its foundations that the *à part* cannot appear. The dialogue must engage itself totally in the struggle for its own continuity if, in fact, dramatic form is to be preserved. And, although comedy and tragedy permeate each other in genuine Drama, as in Kleist's *Amphitryon*, the aside tends readily toward the comic pole. Therefore, Jupiter's "curse the madness that lured me here"[4]—the suggestion of divine tragedy— constantly runs the danger of not being taken seriously because it is the remark of someone who has been duped.

Hebbel's Dramas point with particular clarity to the historical change in the significance of the aside that took place when modern dramaturgy came into being. Rudolf Kassner saw in the heroes of these plays individuals "who had long been by themselves, speechless."[5] In fact, for them the aside is rather a "by-one's-self,"—even an "in-one's-self," a sort of speech without words. Asides are no longer a function of the situation; instead, the situation gives rise to the occasion in which they reveal the inner being of the individual of whom they are already an externalization. Thus, Herod's mad idea is already announced in the seemingly innocent conversation of the first scene, owing to an interpolated "for-one's-self." Judas, a captain, reports to him about the raging fire of the previous night and speaks of a woman who refused to leave the burning house.

> *Herod*: She must have been demented!
> *Judas*:   Possibly
>   Her mind had been upset by pain and grief!
>   Her husband had just died a while before,
>   His body lay still warm upon the bed.
> *Herod* (*aside*): That I will surely tell to Mariamne
>   And watch her while I tell her! (*aloud*) Probably
>   This woman had no child! But if she had,
>   I will take care of it! She shall herself
>   Be buried richly and with royal splendor,
>   She was, it may well be, the queen of women![6]

And in the decisive conversation:

> *Herod*:   If ever I
>   Myself lay dying I could even do
>   What you expect Salome would, prepare
>   A poison in your wine and give it to you,
>   So I should still be sure of you in death!
> *Mariamne*: If you did that, you would no doubt recover!
> *Herod*: Oh no! For I would share this poison with you!
>   But tell me whether you could e'er forgive
>   Such an excess of love as that would be!
> *Mariamne*: If after drinking such a drink I still
>   Had only breath enough for one last word,
>   Then I would curse you with that final word!
>   (*aside*) Yes, all the more, the more I'm sure that I
>   Could reach out for the dagger in my grief
>   To kill myself if death should call you hence:
>   That one can do, not have it done to him![7]

Here the aside does not correct the error of an external situation; in it the conversation with Herod is, rather, carried forward within Mariamne. It reveals her inmost feelings, feelings that do not deny but fundamentally deepen what she says. It is not two different beings that speak in Mariamne—one who dissembles before Herod and one who is really her. She would not betray herself (as Kleist's Jupiter did, e.g.,) if she said everything aloud; but she has feelings that her spirit prevents her from sharing with her consort. And that she must at this point remain silent about her real love for Herod contributes significantly to our understanding of her nature.

Thus, Hebbel's use of the aside anticipates the *monologue intérieur* technique employed by the psychological novelists of the twentieth century; and one can understand why modern dramaturgy allowed itself to be animated by Joyce's school in its extended use of the *à part*. In this sense, Eugene O'Neill's nine-act Drama, *Strange Interlude* (1928), not only records the conversations of its eight heroes but also continually notes their thoughts, which they cannot share because they feel too estranged from one another. This is demonstrated indirectly at the beginning of the last act. For the first time, the inward monologues are silenced when two young lovers face each other — lovers who, for the moment at least, know nothing of the gulf between human beings. But because the *à part* shares equally with the dialogue the responsibility for shaping the form, it loses the right to this designation. It makes sense to speak of the aside only in a space in which, in principle, people speak to one another. Here, however, the *à part* is not a passing self-suppression of the dialogue; it stands autonomous, next to dramatic dialogue, as the psychological report of an epic *I*. Therefore, *Strange Interlude* takes the form of a montage constructed of dramatic and epic parts. The montage requires an epic *I* not simply to provide the psychological insights of the *à part* but also to ensure its formal completeness, because the continuity of the work can no longer be derived from the dialogue itself. If soliloquies followed one another without any dialogue, time would stand still; no epic *I* would hold them on course. But the epic *monteur* of *Strange Interlude* can be understood in terms other than those of the psychological Drama. The naturalistic novelist lives on in him as well, a descendant of Zola, who no longer has a word to put in about his hero — to say nothing of a good word; a descendant who now only registers, machinelike, the outer and inner speech provided him by individuals in the unfree space of genetic and psychological laws.

16. The Epic *I* as Stage Manager: Wilder

Hardly another work of the modern theater is at once so bold in the formal realm and of such moving simplicity in the statement it makes as Thornton Wilder's *Our Town* (1938). In it the melancholy lyric quality that everyday events assume shows Wilder's debt to Chekhov; but his formal innovations represent an attempt to free the Chekhovian heritage from its contradictions and provide it with an adequate form beyond that of the Drama. Chekhov (like Hauptmann and others) did not wish to forgo dramatic form. Therefore, he had to give his heroes at least the beginnings of dramatic life, despite the fact that this life did not unfold in the sphere of conflict and decision. Uniform, uneventful, deeply impersonal, and tedious events became immediate/interpersonal events and acquired the appearance of uniqueness. But, Wilder did not want to prove himself disloyal to his theme for these purely formal reasons. Therefore, he released the action from its dramatic function — that is, allowed it to generate form out of its own inner oppositions. He transferred this responsibility to a new character, the Stage Manager, who stood outside the thematic space in the pivotal position occupied by the narrator. Since, for him, the dramatis personae function as objects of the performance, the fact of performance, which was always hidden in genuine Drama, becomes explicit here.[1] One can speak of the "destruction of illusion" at this point, but the notion, which comes from romantic dramaturgy, may not be borrowed uncritically. In terms of the psychology of reception, dramatic "illusion" designates the homogeneous world of the Drama, its absolute quality.[2] Illusion is destroyed when the structure of the Drama becomes differentiated, when another (supra- or intra-personal) relation cuts across the interpersonal. In both Tieck's "romantic irony" and Wilder's "epic theater," this relationship operates between the subject and the object of consciousness, but with one essential difference: the roles in Tieck's comedy, being projections of the early romantic subject, are conscious of themselves as objects — that is, they become their own objects,* whereas in *Our Town* it is the Stage Manager who is conscious of the roles as roles and, thus, represents a subject-object relationship external to them — precisely that epic relationship existing between the narrator and his object. The result of the romantic's destruction of illusion was to give shape to the actual loss of the world as it was experienced by the now all-powerful *I*. The destruction of illusion in the modern "drama" on the other hand, leads to that aestheticized representation of reality supplied by all epic writing.

Dramatic action is replaced by scenic narrative, the order of which is determined by the Stage Manager. The individual parts do not, as in the Drama, engender one another; they are bound together in a whole by the epic *I* according to a plan that moves beyond individual events to the general. Because of this, the element of tension found in the Drama also recedes; the individual scene no longer carries within it the seed of the next. The exposition, the dramatization of which (i.e., its inclusion in the unfolding action) may never have been as difficult as it was in this case, can retain its epic objectivity here. The first act is called "the Daily Life"[3]: morning, midday, and evening, it briefly depicts the lives of two families. Because these scenes have no dramatic function conferred on them, they are not required to give life the sharp edge of conflictual situations; everything indicates that the day presented, May 7, 1901, is a day like every other. Even the portrayal of the two neighboring families is based on their representativeness; neither the doctor's nor the editor's family has special or characteristic features: each has two children, a boy and a girl, each has problems common to every family, and each conveys details in its conversations that stand for a thousand other families. "Love and Marriage" is the title of the second act. It is July 7, 1904, the day on which the doctor's son and the editor's daughter marry. It too is a day that begins like all others. Then come the wedding preparations. To explain the wedding, the Stage Manager reaches back into the past and grants new scenic presence to the conversation in which George and

Emily discover their mutual feelings. Following this conversation comes another, also from the past, in which George's parents discuss the impending marriage. Next comes the wedding ceremony, again presented not as something singular and immediate but as an event the advent and significance of which is common to the life of almost every individual. The Stage Manager says, "There are a lot of things to be said about a wedding; there are a lot of thoughts that go on during a wedding. We can't get them all into *one* wedding, naturally, and especially not into a wedding at Grover's Corners, where they're awfully plain and short. In this wedding I play the minister. That gives me the right to say a few more things about it."[4] The representative character of the action is so exposed that the Stage Manager can add a verbal supplement to the scenic presentation when the latter is insufficient. The same thing occurs in the third act, which is about death. Nine years later, in the summer of 1913, Emily dies while giving birth to her second child. She is buried in Grover's Corners cemetery.

But the Stage Manager does not simply take over the task of ensuring a formal whole—a task that had belonged to the action. In him the thematic that had produced the crisis in the Drama at the turn of the century precipitates as form. The earlier fragmentation of interpersonal relationships had produced a paradoxical situation for the dialogue: the more unstable its existential underpinnings became, the more obliged it was to resolve in dialogic form the alienated matter that came from extradialogic spaces—from the past[5] or social conditions.[6] Here, the Stage Manager takes over from the dialogic action the task of presenting this objective material. The intrathematic, epic distance that Ibsen's characters maintained regarding the past and that Hauptmann's characters maintained regarding the political and economic conditions of their lives—despite dramatic form—achieves formal expression in the epic posture of the Stage Manager. He replaces the mediating figures found within the action of the transitional plays of Strindberg and Hauptmann: the company director, Hummel,[7] and the social scientist, Loth.[8]

The temporal context for *Our Town's* three widely separated acts, along with the past and the future, is given epic presentation in the incidental information added by the Stage Manager. His description of the surrounding world is even more significant, however: the town of Grover's Corners, with its geographical, political, cultural, and religious conditions. What the naturalist playwright, in an effort doomed to failure, had painstakingly tried to translate into immediate/interpersonal events is here reported to the public by the Stage Manager, by a "university professor," and by the editor, who is also part of the action. This information is provided in the form of an introduction and between the first three scenes. The spectator is instructed in ironic but precise scientific fashion about the background upon which the lives of the two families will be played out—but only as representatives of the life of the town. Even though this play preserves the naturalist desire to expose the surrounding world as the determining factor in individual existence, it also tries to rid the dialogic realm of the objective elements that had constantly threatened to transpose the dialogue of the transitional plays into epic description. The absence of a stage set and properties can be understood as the external signs of this effort. The objective can appear only in the Stage Manager's report; the stage itself must remain free to accommodate the already endangered and reduced interpersonal events. Because of this epic shaping of external conditions, the dialogue in *Our Town* achieves a transparence and purity that only the lyric Drama has possessed in the post neoclassical period. Thus, Wilder's epic theater proves to be more than a renunciation of the Drama; it is also an attempt to prepare a new site and an epic framework for the very substance of the Drama—the dialogue.

The degree to which the dialogue is called into question from within becomes apparent in the last act, however, when Wilder manages to resubmerge both the formal principle and the insight that led to it in the thematic. Emily, carried to her grave, longs to be with the living and not among the dead. In vain the dead try to dissuade her. She dares to face the painful disappointment she has been told awaits her and asks the Stage Manager if she can relive at least one day of her life—her twelfth birthday. The Stage Manager's epic freedom to reach back in time and make the past present once more[9] is transformed into an almost godlike freedom at this point: he can revivify the past for the dead. This day is no longer presented for the spectators but for an onlooking dramatis persona; and the narrator's epic distance from the life he depicts becomes simply the distance between the dead and life. Just as in Hofmannsthal's early work, and frequently thereafter,[10] the perennial self-alienation of the individual is illustrated from the perspective of dying or death, the only vantage point that could really justify such distancing of the individual from himself. The image the dead have of the living thus proves to be the deathly picture that today's individual has of himself.

> *Emily*: . . . Live people don't understand do they?
> *Mrs. Gibbs*: No, dear—not very much.
> *Emily*: They're sort of shut up in little boxes aren't they?[11]

This is one insight that death makes possible. The other can be understood only by inverting it; only then does it become a real insight.

> *Emily*: . . . Why should that be painful: [That is, her return.]
> *Stage Manager*: You not only live it; but you watch yourself living it.[12]

Although estranged as the experience of a dead person, if these lines did not express a basic experience of people living today, the tragic aspect of the next scene, which involves Emily both as participating child and as onlooking woman would be incomprehensible to the spectator. The fact that Emily also continually sees herself is the obverse of that blindness she recognizes in the living: "everybody's inevitable self-preoccupation." In this statement, taken from one of his letters, Wilder joins the two and makes a reference to Chekhov. "Chekhov's plays are always exhibiting this: Nobody hears what anyone else says. Everybody walks in a self-centered dream. . . . It is certainly one of the principle points that the Return to the Birthday makes."[13] Wilder's renunciation of dramatic form — of dialogue as the sole mode of expression — can also be understood on the basis of this insight.

17. The Play of Time: Wilder

"It is high time I should come out into the open air again. . . . Nearly three years in detention — five years in prison — eight years in the gallery up there." This is the manner in which time is presented in Ibsen's analytical Drama; it is named and calculated.[1] But the possibility of expressing the essence of time, its duration, its passing, and the changes it produces, was denied Ibsen the dramatist, because such expression is possible only in a literary form that allows the joint, thematic, and formal representation of two different points in time. Their quantitative and qualitative difference is the only evidence that time, in its all-transforming flight, leaves behind. But the temporal structure of the Drama is one of absolute linear sequentiality.[2] In it only the (always) present moment is visible, a moment turned toward the future, of course — one that destroys itself for the sake of the future moment. The accord between action and temporal movement expressed by this sort of tightened focus on the (always) present is not the same as that sense of time generated by Ibsen's protagonists, however. The idle reflection that marks them seems to lift them out of the flow of time and allows them their first real opportunity to give it thematic expression. Ibsen takes this into account by dramatizing only the last chapter in the life story of his protagonists and by unfolding this scenically presented finale analytically, in the form of conversations. The simultaneous epic representation of different points in time is, therefore, at least achieved thematically, even if at the expense of the dramatic action and its absolute linear presence, which, because of the all-dominant analysis, are no longer "dramatic." Of course, this critique is not applicable to the dramaturgic tradition with which Ibsen is frequently, but erroneously, associated. Dramatists have regularly found themselves faced with material whose temporal dimension made it appear unsuitable for the Drama. If they did not want to give it up entirely (as was the case for Grillparzer and his Napoleon material), they were obliged to safeguard it for the Drama by concentrating on its end phase. Schiller's *Mary Stuart* is a classic example of this practice, and it makes the difference with regard to Ibsen absolutely clear. Schiller was hardly concerned with providing a retrospective narrative of the Scottish queen's life, and even less concerned about it serving as an example of the thematically presented past of an individual. Instead, in this last chapter, the whole struggle between Mary and Elizabeth is present. Indeed, it is fought out here for the first time. One would be interpreting Schiller in terms of Sophocles or even Ibsen if one assumed that, when the curtain goes up, everything has already been decided and that the death warrant has already been signed.[3]

Time as such first became problematic in that postneoclassical era referred to as bourgeois—an era for which Ibsen will no doubt always be considered the most representative dramatist. The first major document concerning this preoccupation with time was not a play, however; it was a late manifestation of the novel of development, namely, Flaubert's *L'education sentimentale*.[4] And the high point of such concern was reached in the oeuvre of Flaubert's only student: Proust's *A la recherche du temps perdu*. Proust's experience of the tragic dialectic between happiness as fulfilled desire and time as a transforming power is one of the major themes of this novel. Proust was struck by the painful awareness that all fulfillment comes essentially too late, since, as a person strives toward the object of his desire, he is transformed by time and the fulfillment no longer corresponds with the original wish. Instead, it meets only emptiness. This is why, according to Proust, only the unexpected, that which was never desire's goal, can really make one happy.*

This sort of reflectively experienced equation of being and time can only be given shape by the novel. And it is not without justification that modern literature has been accused of a "complete disorientedness" that poses the problem of "representing development and the gradual passing of time in dramatic terms."[5] But it would not be appropriate to lump "dramatic" and "scenic" together and thereby deny both the Drama and the theater in general access to time as a theme, particularly since even a single work, if it is successful in providing a dialogic-scenic representation of time, witnesses to the theoretical possibility of such representation as well. And Thornton Wilder's one-act, *The Long Christmas Dinner* (1931), must certainly be regarded as a success of this sort.

The motif of time, of its passing and standing still, surfaces regularly at the Bayard family table during this "long Christmas dinner."

> Anyway, no time passes as slowly as this when you're waiting for your urchins to grow up and settle down to business. . . . I don't want time to go any faster, thank you.[6]
> But darling, the time will pass so fast that you'll hardly know I'm gone.[7]
> Isn't there anything I can do? . . . No, dear. Only time, only the passing of time can help in these things.[8]
> Goodbye, darling. Don't grow up too fast. . . . stay just as you are.[9]
> Time certainly goes very fast in a great new country like this. . . . Well, the time must be passing very slowly in Europe with this dreadful, dreadful war going on.[10]

Isn't there anything I can do? . . . No, no. Only time, only the passing of time can help in these things.[11]
Time passes so slowly here that it stands still, that's what the trouble
is. . . . I'm going somewhere where time passes, my God![12]
How slowly time passes without any young people in the house.[13]
I can't stand it. I can't stand it any more. . . . It's the *thoughts*, it's
the thought of what might have been here. And the feeling about this
house of the years *grinding away.*[14]

There are not just verbal references to time, however. Dramaturgic devices, some of which are borrowed from the cinema but which attain their greatest efficacy in the theater, are used to evoke the passage of time in almost abstract purity and allow it to be experienced without mediation. The opening stage directions indicate that "ninety years are to be traversed in this play which represents in accelerated motion ninety Christmas dinners in the Bayard house-hold." The expression "in accelerated motion" should not be taken literally, how-ever, because even though ninety years are spanned in the Christmas dinner por-trayed on stage, the normal rhythm of movement and speech is maintained throughout. The fast-motion shot is not used here in the mechanical fashion of the movies, where it usually serves comic, rarely documentary, purposes (e.g., the portrayal of slow-moving events) and never brings the passage of time into sharp focus. The cinema would use montage rather than fast motion to solve the problem of how to depict the permutations of ninety Christmases. It would juxta-pose clips of individual Christmas celebrations, separated by years or decades. Their diversity would then speak for the transforming power of time but only insofar as it came to expression through such spatial deconstruction and only in terms of the images presented. Wilder, too, uses montage, and in his role as epic narrator places numerous segments next to one another, but—this time as dramatist—he also goes beyond the cinematic by joining these temporally dis-parate fragments in a dramatic whole that gives the impression of a single—although "long"—Christmas dinner. It is only this second step that transforms the epic montage into an absolute dramatic event and thereby grants the con-tinuity that makes possible the immediate time/experience mentioned earlier. It is as if the periods of time that had fallen into the interstices of the montage were forced out of hiding when the mass of fragments achieved dramatic unity. These time periods were themselves thereby bound together in a unified temporal movement that does not constitute but, rather, accompanies the "long Christmas dinner" as an independent entity.

When the montage, which encompasses ninety years, is transformed into a dramatic event, the result is a division of the temporal flow into two movements: a formal movement that corresponds to the time of the performance, and a sec-ond movement, which is imposed on the content by the original montage. This duality, which is natural in the epic, and which Günther Müller has formulated as the conceptual pair "narrative time/narrated time," has a particular effect within the framework of the Drama.* Since the two tempi do not correspond, the result is an "estrangement effect," in Brecht's sense of the term: the flow of time, which, in the Drama as well as in active life, is immanent in an action and therefore not at all present to consciousness as an independent entity, is suddenly experienced as something new because of the dissociation of things that ought to be identical. Just as the duration of time can be grasped only when spatialized as the difference between two points in time—as a span of time—it seems that the unfolding of time, too, can be delineated only as the difference between two temporal movements, each immanent in the action, that have been laid parallel to each other.

This difference in temporal movements, which can be traced back to the two phases in which the work arose (montage and dramatization), is the formal principle underlying *The Long Christmas Dinner*. Everything points to the same desire—that is, to allow the passage of time to be experienced in the most intense manner possible, by conveying it through the difference just mentioned. In terms of the action, the ninety years correspond to that "decline of a family" previously given epic portrayal by Thomas Mann. After the constructive life and internal unity of the first generation comes the estrangement of brothers and sisters, the dissatisfaction with small town life, and the flight from family tradition. On the dramatic level, this process contrasts with the Christmas dinner which, like all such festive occasions, makes time stand still, changes temporal movement into repetition, and leads to remembrance of the past. Thus, the static condition of the second event not only constitutes the desired opposite of the first but also draws attention to the latter by calling forth memories:

> *Charles*: . . . it certainly is a keen, cold morning. I used to go skat-
> ing with Father on mornings like this and Mother would come back
> from church saying—
> *Genevieve (dreamily)*: I know: saying "Such a splendid sermon. I cried
> and cried."
> *Leonora*: Why did she cry, dear?
> *Genevieve*: That generation all cried at sermons. It was their way.
> *Leonora*: Really, Genevieve?
> *Genevieve*: They had had to go since they were children and I suppose
> sermons reminded them of their fathers and mothers, just as
> Christmas dinners do us. Especially in an old house like this.[15]

This dual function of the repetition becomes even clearer in the conversations. While the ninety-year time passage is expressed through brief references to new and different incidents, the same, almost formulaic sentences are repeated during the Christmas dinner. The sermon is praised again and again,[16] a traditional turn of phrase is used as wine is poured,[17] the rheumatism of an acquaintance is discussed, or the maid is asked to serve. Through these repetitions, the Christmas event, which does not change, separates itself from the process that encompasses ninety years. But at the same time, the event gives expression to the process whenever names change (that of the pastor, of the sick acquaintance, of the maid) and also because it is itself a repetition—one that would be incomprehensible without the interim movement of time. The dramatis personae too, reveal the constant duality of change and stability, when the four generations that succeed one another are contrasted with the static figure of the "poor relation" who lives in the house and who changes only once. And finally, this duality is the basis for the scenic style as well. The Christmas dinner is set realistically: "the dining-room of the Bayard home. Close to the footlights a long dining table is handsomely spread for Christmas dinner. The carver's place with a great turkey before it is at the spectator's right. A door, left back, leads into the hall." But this realism is permeated by the symbols of temporal coming and going: "at the extreme left, by the proscenium pillar, is a strange portal trimmed with garlands of fruits and flowers. Directly opposite is another edged and hung with black velvet. The portals denote birth and death."[18] And since these two portals remain in front of and unconnected with the realistic set, the "natural" performance of the actors—"natural" despite the absence of props—is regularly transformed into symbolic performance: the birth of the children is represented by their entry through the fruit- and flower-bedecked portal; a serious illness of long duration is indicated by having the sick person get up from the table and move closer to, then hesitate in front of the portal hung in black; aging is symbolized by a white-haired wig donned almost without notice; finally, death, by an exit through the black portal. It is this simple scenographic symbolism (a symbolism that, because it is epic/representational, contrasts with dramatic illusionism) that finally reveals the true nature of the play, which, up to this point, has been regarded from a technical point of view as dramatized montage: it is a secular mystery play about time.

18. Memory: Miller

Arthur Miller's evolution from imitator to innovator, which occurred between the publication of his first two works, is the clearest example of that general change in style that both unites and separates the turn-of-the-century dramatists and those of the present: the emergence out of dramatic form of a new formal structure for those epic elements that had previously only been given thematic expression. If this process, which is central to the developmental history of the modern theater, has, up to this point, been presented mainly in terms of a comparison between the two periods—by contrasting Ibsen and Pirandello, Chekhov and Wilder, Hauptmann and Brecht—in Miller's case, as with Strindberg's earlier, it can be illuminated by the works of a single author.

In *All My Sons* (1947), Miller tried to preserve Ibsen's analytical approach to social dramaturgy by transferring it into the American present. An inexorable analysis slowly reveals the long-hidden crime committed by the head of the Keller family: his delivery of defective airplane parts to the Army, a deed that involves him in another — the suicide of his son Larry — which has also been kept secret. All the secondary aspects of the action needed to narrate the past as a dramatic event are at hand — the return of Larry's former fiancée and her brother, for example. Their father, an employee of Keller's, was wrongfully imprisoned for Keller's offense. Even Ibsen's often heavy-handed use of the set is preserved in this work: an element of the decor gives visible presence to the ongoing internal effects of the past, while also laboring to symbolize the deeper meaning of the play. In this case it is the tree that long ago had been planted for Larry. Felled by the previous night's storm, its shattered stump stands in the backyard where the play is set. If *All My Sons* had not been followed by *Death of a Salesman*, it might possibly have been discussed here as an example of Ibsen's powerful influence in the Anglo-Saxon world, an influence that begins with G[eorge] B[ernard] Shaw and lives on today. As it is, however, the play can be regarded as a work from his apprentice years, as if Miller, engaged in giving scenic form to a "wasted lifetime"[1] and in particular to a traumatic past, had, while following in Ibsen's footsteps, come to understand the manner in which dramatic form resists this thematic and the costs attached to making the former serve the latter. What was shown here earlier with respect to *John Gabriel Borkman* must have become clear to Miller as he worked on *All My Sons*: the contradiction between a remembered past conveyed by the thematic and the spatial-temporal present postulated by dramatic form; the resulting need to contrive a supplementary action with which to motivate the analysis; and, the disharmony produced by the fact that this second set of events dominates the stage while the real "action" emerges only in the confessions of the characters.

In his second play, Miller tries to escape these contradictions by surrendering dramatic form. Fundamental here is the fact that he does not disguise the analysis as action. The past is no longer forced into open discussion by a dramatic conflict; the dramatis personae are no longer portrayed as masters of the past to satisfy a formal principle when in fact they are its helpless victims. Instead, the past achieves representation in the same way that it emerges in life itself — of its own accord, in the *mémoire involontaire* (Proust). Therefore, the past remains a subjective experience and can create no illusory bridges between the individuals whom the analysis brings together — individuals whom it had left in lifelong separation. Thus, instead of an interpersonal action that would call forth discussion of the past, the present generated by the thematic discloses the psychic state of the individual overpowered by memory. Willy Loman, an aging salesman, is presented in this manner; the play begins as he slips completely under the thrall of memory. The family has recently begun to notice that he talks to himself. In fact, he is actually talking to them, not in the real present but in the past he remembers, which no longer leaves him alone. The present of the play is constituted by the forty-eight hours that follow Loman's unexpected return from a business trip. The past had continuously gotten the better of him as he sat behind the steering wheel of his car. He tries in vain to arrange a transfer to the New York office of the company he has represented for several decades; his constant references to the past reveal the state he is in, and he is fired. Finally, Loman commits suicide so that his family can benefit from his insurance policy.

This actional framework, which is situated in the present, has little to do with that found in Ibsen's Drama or even in *All My Sons*. It is not a dramatic event that closes on itself; and it does not require that the past be conjured up in dialogue. The scene between Loman and his employer is characteristic in this respect. The latter is unwilling to join in a conversation that would give presence to the salesman's career and to his own father, who is supposed to have been favorably disposed toward Loman. He finds an excuse to leave the room and hurries out, leaving Loman alone with his ever more vivid memories.

These memories in turn create a means (one already long familiar to the cinema under the name flashback) of introducing the past into the space beyond dialogue. The scene shifts constantly in the play staged for Loman by his *mémoire involontaire*. Unlike the Ibsenesque courtroom procedure, remembrance occurs without being spoken of—that is, entirely on the level of form.[2] The protagonist regards himself in the past and, as self-remembering *I*, is absorbed into the formal subjectivity of the work. The scene presents only the epic object of this subjectivity, the remembered *I* itself, the salesman in the past, his conversations with the members of his family. The latter are no longer independent dramatis personae; they emerge as references to the central *I*, in the same manner as do the character projections in expressionist dramaturgy. One can readily grasp the epic nature of this play of memory by comparing it to the "play within a play" as it appears in the Drama. Hamlet's play, which presents the imagined past in order to "catch the conscience of the king,"[3]* is built into the action in the form of an episode. It constitutes a closed sphere that leaves the surrounding world of action intact. Because this second play is a thematic piece that does not need to conceal the fact of its performance, the time and place of the two actions are not in conflict—the dramatic unities and the absoluteness of the events are maintained. In *Death of a Salesman*, on the other hand, the past is not played as a thematic episode; the present and its action constantly overflow into the play of the past. No troupe of actors enters; without saying a word, the characters can become actors enacting themselves because the alternation between immediate/personal and past/remembered events is anchored in the epic principle of form operative here. The dramatic unities are likewise abolished— indeed, abolished in the most radical sense: memory signifies not only a multiplicity of times and places but also the absolute loss of their identity. The temporal-spatial present of the action is not simply relativized in terms of other presents; on the contrary, it is in itself relative. Therefore, there is no real change in the setting, and, at the same time, it is perpetually transformed. The salesman's house remains on stage, but in the scenes remembered, its walls are of no concern—as is the case with memory, which has no temporal or spatial limits. This relativity of the present becomes particularly clear in those transitional scenes that belong to the outer as well as the inner reality. Such is the situation in the first act when the memory figure, Ben, Willy's brother, appears on stage while he and his neighbor, Charley, are playing cards:

> *Willy*: I'm awfully tired Ben.
> *Charley*: Good, keep playing; you'll sleep better. Did you call me Ben?
> *Willy*: That's funny. For a second there you reminded me of my brother Ben.[4]

The salesman says nothing that indicates he sees his dead brother in front of him. His appearance could be a hallucination, but only within dramatic form, which by definition excludes the inner world. Yet, in this play, present reality and the reality of the past achieve simultaneous representation. Because Loman is reminded of his brother, the latter appears on stage: memory has been incorporated into the principle underlying scenic form. Because interior monologue (dialogue with a figure evoked by memory), stands side by side with dialogue, the result is a Chekhovian speaking at cross purposes:

> *Ben*: Is Mother living with you?
> *Willy*: No, she died a long time ago.
> *Charley*: Who?
> *Ben*: That's too bad. Fine specimen of a lady, Mother.
> *Willy* (*to Charley*): Heh?
> *Ben*: I'd hoped to see the old girl.
> *Charley*: Who died?
> *Ben*: Heard anything from Father, have you?
> *Willy* (*unnerved*): What do you mean, who died?
> *Charley*: . . . What're you talkin' about?[5]

To give dramatic form to this sort of continual misunderstanding, Chekhov needed the supporting theme supplied by deafness.[6] In *Death of a Salesman*, on the other hand, it arises formally out of the side-by-side existence of the two worlds. Their concurrent representation sets in motion the new principle of form. Its advantage over the Chekhovian technique is obvious. The supporting theme, the symbolic character of which remains vague, does introduce the possibility of mutual misunderstanding, but it also hides the real source of this misunderstanding—the individual's preoccupation with himself and with a remembered past, a past that can appear as such only after the formal principle of the Drama is abolished.

It is this past, once again present, that finally opens the salesman's eyes as he desperately tries to understand his own misfortune and, even more, the failed career of his elder son [Biff]. While sitting across from his sons in a restaurant, a scene from the past suddenly surfaces in his memory and, therefore, becomes visible to the audience as well: his son finds him in a Boston hotel room with his mistress. At this point, Loman can understand why his son later wandered from job to job and why he thwarted his career prospects by stealing: he wanted to punish his father.

In *Death of a Salesman*, Miller did not want to reveal this secret, the failure of the father (which was borrowed from Ibsen and central to *All My Sons*), through a judicial procedure invented for the sake of form. He gave credence to Balzac's comment, under the sign of which both Ibsen's and Miller's characters stand: "We all die unknown."[7] Because memory takes its place beside the (always) present of the dialogue, which constitutes the sole representational possibility of the Drama, the play successfully presents a dramatic paradox: the past of a number of characters is given visible presence but only for a single consciousness. In contrast to the analysis that is part of the thematic in Ibsen, this play of the past, founded on the principle of form, has no effect on the other characters. For the son, this scene remains a permanent and heavily guarded secret. He is unable to reveal to anyone the shattering effect it has had on his life. Because of this, his mute hatred breaks into the open neither before his father's suicide nor after it. And in the "Requiem," which closes the play, it is precisely the unsuspecting quality of the remarks made by Linda, the salesman's wife, that makes them so moving.

> *Linda*: Forgive me, dear. I can't cry, I don't know what it is, but I can't cry. I don't understand it. Why did you ever do that? Help me, Willy, I can't cry. It seems to me that you're just on another trip. I keep expecting you. Willy, dear, I can't cry. Why did you do it? I search and I search and I search, and I can't understand it. . . .

The Curtain Falls[8]

In Lieu of an Afterword

The history of modern dramaturgy has no final act; the curtain has not been low-ered on it yet. Therefore, the ideas that bring this discussion to a temporary end are by no means its conclusion. The time for summing up has no more arrived than the time in which new norms can be established. To prescribe what the modern drama should be is, in any case, not the responsibility of a theory of that drama. What is appropriate here is simply insight into that which has been written, and an attempt to give it theoretical formulation. The goal is to identify new forms, since the history of art is not determined by ideas but by the process that gives form to these ideas. Dramatists have succeeded in hammering out a new form based on today's altered thematics—will this form produce results in the future? Of course, whatever is formal instead of thematic always contains the possibility of its future tradition within itself. However, the historical trans-formation of the relationship between subject and object has called not only dra-matic form into question but the notion of tradition as well. And our epoch, for which originality is everything, has seen only imitations. Therefore, to make a new style possible, the crisis of the Drama as well as that of tradition will have to be resolved.

Crucial insights for this study have been gleaned from Hegel's aesthetics; E[mil] Staiger's *Grundbegriffe der Poetik*; G[eorg] Lukács's essay "Zur Soziologie der modernen Dramas," and T[heodor] W. Adorno's *Philosophy of Modern Music*.

Zurich, September 1956

For the 1963 Edition

This study was written ten years ago. That explains the choice of examples, which would probably not be entirely the same if the book were to be written today. Nonetheless, if one were to demand that this new edition treat the dramaturgy of the last decade as well, it would be to misunderstand its intention and regard it as a history of the modern drama. The plays included as examples have been read in an effort to discover the developmental terms of the modern drama. Therefore, the text has not been expanded, only slightly revised.

Göttingen, February 1963

Notes

Notes

Foreword

1. One of the three German editions has sold over 100,000 copies. The book has been translated into Italian (1962), Slovakian (1969), Swedish (1972), Polish (1976), and French (1983). It has inspired several long reviews. See, for example, Jacob Steiner, "Theorie des modernen Dramas," in *orbis litterarum* 13, issue 1–2 (1958): 178–85, and Thomas Metscher, "Dialektik und Formalismus. Kritik des literaturwissenschaftlichen Idealismus am Beispiel Peter Szondis," in Th. M., *Kunst und sozialer Prozeß* (Cologne, 1977), pp. 15–48.

2. "Die Theorie des Romans zumal hat durch Tiefe und Elan der Konzeption ebenso wie durch die nach damaligen Begriffen außerordentliche Dichte und Intensität der Darstellung einen Maßstab philosophischer Ästhetik aufgerichtet, der seitdem nicht wieder verloren ward." Theodore W. Adorno, *Gesammelte Schriften* 11 (Frankfurt, 1974): 250.

3. See, for instance, J. M. Bernstein, *The Philosophy of the Novel. Lukács, Marxism and the Dialectics of Form* (Minneapolis, 1984).

4. Paul de Man, *Blindness and Insight. Essays in the Rhetoric of Contemporary Criticism*, 2d rev. ed. (Minneapolis, 1983), p. 52.

5. Georg Lukács, *The Theory of the Novel* (Cambridge, Mass. 1971), p. 29. Henceforth cited within the text.

6. Peter Szondi, *On Textual Understanding and Other Essays*, trans. Harvey Mendelsohn; (Minneapolis, 1986), p. 63.

7. The "Don Carlos Letters" are contained in *Friedrich Schiller. Plays "Intrigue and Love" and "Don Carlos," The German Library* 15, Walter Hinderer, ed. trans. Charles E. Passage, A. Leslie, and Jeanne R. Wilson (New York, 1983). The quote cited can be found on p. 312. The letters are henceforth cited in the text.

8. Lukács, *The Theory of the Novel*, p. 74–75.

9. de Man, *Blindness and Insight*, p. 56.

10. See my introduction to Géza von Molnár's *Romantic Vision, Ethical Context. Novalis and Artistic Autonomy* (Minneapolis, 1986).

11. For a different understanding of mimesis, one that actually juxtaposes the meaning of this term with that of imitation, see Luiz Costa Lima, *Control of the Imaginary*, forthcoming from Minnesota.

12. Georg Friedrich Wilhelm Hegel, *Ästhetik I* (Frankfurt, n.d.), pp. 71–76. The quote appears on p. 74.

13. Szondi, *Textual Understanding*, pp. 66–67.

14. Ibid, p. 140.

15. Ibid, p. 139.

16. de Man, *Blindness and Insight*, pp. 219–20.

17. See Wolfgang Schivelbusch, *Sozialistisches Drama nach Brecht. Drei Modelle: Peter Hacks–Heiner Müller–Hartmut Lange* (Neuwied, 1974), and Jochen Schulte-Sasse, "Hartmut Lange," in Dietrich Weber, ed., *Deutsche Literatur der Gegenwart* 2 (Stuttgart, 1977), pp. 356–83.

18. Reiner Steinweg, ed. *Brechts Modell der Lehrstücke. Zeugnissse. Diskussion, Erfahrungen* (Frankfurt, 1976), p. 51. In a series of publications, Steinweg nearly single-handedly unearthed and interpreted Brecht's *Lehrstücktheorie* and revived its practice. See also Reiner Steinweg, *Das Lehrstück. Brechts Theorie einer politisch-ästhetischen Erziehung* (Stuttgart, 1972), and Bertolt Brecht, *Die Maßnahme. Kritische Augabe mit einer Spielanleitung*, Reiner Steinweg, ed. (Frankfurt, 1972).

Introduction: Historical Aesthetics and Genre-Based Poetics

1. Aristotle, *Poetics* [trans. I. Bywater, in *The Students Oxford Aristotle* 6, ed. W. D. Ross (Oxford, 1942)], 1456a.

2. See Goethe, *Über Epische und Dramatische Dichtung* [in *Werke* 12 (Hamburg, 1953), pp. 249–51], and Schiller's letter to Goethe of December 26, 1789.

3. [J. W. G.] Hegel, *Sämtliche Werke, Jubiläumsausgabe* 7, (Stuttgart, 1939), p. 303. [For a slightly different English version of this text, see *Hegel's Logic*, 3d ed., trans. W. Wallace (Oxford, 1975), p. 190.]

4. *Werke* 7, p. 302 [*Logic*, p. 189].

5. T[heodor] W. Adorno, *Philosophie der neuen Musik* (Tubingen, 1949), p. 28 [*The Philosophy of Modern Music*, trans. A. Mitchell (New York, 1973), p. 42. See esp. editorial note.]

6. [Zurich, 1946], see p. [9].

7. G[eorg] Lukács, *Die Theorie des Romans* (Berlin, 1920), p. 36 [*The Theory of the Novel*, trans. A. Bostock (Cambridge, Mass., 1971), p. 50].

8. R. Petsch, *Wesen und Formen der Erzählkunst* (Halle, 1943).

I. The Drama

1. In relation to the following discussion see Hegel, *Vorlesungen über die Asthetik*, in *Werke* 14, p. 479 f. [G. W. F. Hegel, *Aesthetics: Lectures on Fine Art* 2, trans. T. M. Knox (Oxford, 1975), p. 1158 f.].

2. See the discussion of dramatic style in Staiger *Grundbegriffe* [p. 143 ff.].

II. The Drama in Crisis

1. Ibsen

1. Hölderlin, *Sämtliche Werke, Grosse Stuttgarter Ausgabe* 2, part 1, ed. Friedriche Beissner (Stuttgart, 1951), p. 373.

2. Aristotle, *Poetics*, 1452a–1452b; see also Peter Szondi, *Versuch über das Tragische* (Frankfurt, 1961), p. 65ff.

3. [*Oedipus the King*, trans. David Grene (Chicago, 1942), p. 353.]

4. *John Gabriel Borkman* [trans. William Archer (1907), repr. in *Henrik Ibsen: The Last Plays* (New York, 1959), p. 81.].

5. [Ibid., p. 113.]

6. [Ibid., p. 125.]

7. [Ibid., p. 84.]

8. [Ibid., p. 114]

9. [Ibid., p. 83.]

10. [Ibid., p. 86.]

11. [Ibid., p. 113.]

12. [Ibid., p. 140.]

13. [Ibid., pp. 125–26.]

14. [Ibid., p. 140.]

15. [Ibid., p. 149.]

16. Lukács, *Theorie des Romans*, p. 127 [*Theory of the Novel*, p. 121].

17. Ibid., p. 135 [p. 126].

18. Ibid. [pp.. 126–27].

19. See R. M. Rilke, *Die Aufzeichnungen des Malta Laurids Brigge* (Leipzig, 1927), pp. 98–102 [*The Notebooks of Malta Laurids Brigge* (New York, 1958), pp. 74–76].

20. See Szondi, *Versuch über das Tragische*, p. 108 f.

21. [Rilke], *Aufzeichnungen*, p. 101 [*Notebooks*, pp. 75–76].

22. Cited in G[eorg] Lukács, *Zur Soziologie des modernen Dramas*, Archiv fur Sozialwissenschaft und Sozialpolitik 38 (1914). See also *Schriften zur Literatursoziologie*, ed. P. Ludz (Neuwied, 1961), pp. 261–95.

2. Chekhov

1. [Chekhov, *The Three Sisters*, trans. A. MacAndrew, in *Twentieth Century Russian Drama* (New York, 1963), p. 67.]

2. [Ibid., p. 44.]

3. [Ibid., p. 57.]

4. [Ibid.]

5. [Ibid., p. 34.]

6. [Ibid., p. 47.]

7. [Ibid., p. 77.]

8. Lukács, *Zur Soziologie des modernen Dramas*, p. 678 ff.

9. Ibid., p. 679.

10. [*Three Sisters*, p. 43.]

11. [Ibid., pp. 52–53.]

3. Strindberg

1. Strindberg, *Samalde Skrifter* 18. Cited in C. E. Dahlstrom, *Strindberg's Dramatic Expressionism* (Ann Arbor, 1930), p. 99.

2. [*The Father*, trans. Arvid Paulson, in Strindberg, *Seven Plays* (New York, 1960), p. 29.]

3. See pp. 9–10.

4. [*The Father*, p. 45.]

5. [Ibid.]

6. Rilke, *Aufzeichnungen*, p. 101 [*Notebooks*, p. 76].

7. [*The Great Highway*, trans. Arvid Paulson, in Strindberg, *Eight Expressionist Plays* (New York, 1972), pp. 414–15.]

8. See Dahlstorm, *Strindberg's Dramatic Expressionism*, pp. 49 ff., 124 ff.

9. [*To Damascus*, trans. Arvid Paulson, in Strindberg, *Eight Expressionist Plays*, p. 141.]

10. Ibid., p. 117.]

11. [*A Dream Play*, trans. E. Sprigge, in *Six Plays of Strindberg* (New York, 1955), p. 220.]

12. [Ibid., p. 213.]

13. [Ibid., p. 246.]

14. [Ibid., p. 226.]

15. [Ibid., p. 230.]

16. [*The Ghost Sonata*, in *Six Plays of Strindberg*, trans. E. Sprigge, p. 274.]

17. [Ibid., p. 284.]

18. [Ibid., p. 297.]

4. Maeterlinck

1. *Les aveugles*, in *Théâtre* 1 (Brussels, 1910) [*The Blind*, trans. R. Hovey, in *The Plays of Maurice Maeterlinck* 1 (Chicago, 1895), p. 265].

2. [Ibid., p. 266].

3. [Ibid., p. 277].

4. [Ibid., p. 267].

5. [Ibid., p. 292].

6. *Intérieur*, in *Théâtre* 2 [*Home*, trans. R. Hovey, *Maeterlinck*, 2d ser. (Chicago, 1896), p. 168].

7. [Ibid., p. 182.]

8. [Ibid., p. 174.]

5. Hauptmann

1. *Die Weber*, in *Gesammelte Werke* 1 (Berlin, 1917) [*The Weavers*, trans. C. Mueller, in *Masterpieces of Modern German Theatre*, ed. R. Corrigan (New York, 1967), p. 211].

2. Ibid., p. 384 [p. 219].

Part Two
Transition: A Theory of Stylistic Change

1. G[eorg] Lukács, *Theorie des Romans*, p. 127. [*Theory of the Novel*, p. 121]

2. [G. W. F.] Hegel, *Vorlesungen über die Asthetik*, in *Sämtliche Werke* 14, p. 324. [*Aesthetics*, p. 1039].

3. See Peter Szondi, "Friedrich Schlegel und die romantische Ironie. Mit einer Beilage über Ludwig Tieck," in *Satz und Gegensatz* (Frankfurt, 1964). [The English version of this essay can be found in Peter Szondi, *On Textual Understanding* (Minneapolis, 1986), chap. 4.]

4. E[mil] Staiger, *Grundbegriffe der Poetik*, p. [61].

5. R[udolph] Kassner, "Erinnerungen an Hofmannsthal," in *Das physiognomische Weltbild* (Munich, 1930), p. 257.

III. Rescue Attempts

6. Naturalism

1. See pp. 23.

7. The Conversation Play

1. See E[mil] Staiger, "Der Schwierige," in *Meisterwerke deutscher Sprache* (Zurich, 1943).

8. The One-Act Play

1. G[eorg] Lukács, *Zur Soziologie des modernen Dramas*, p. 161.
2. See p. 25.
3. Strindberg, "Der Einakter," in *Elf Einakter* (Munich, 1918), p. 340.
4. [Friedrich] Schelling, "Philosophische Briefe über Dogmatismus und Kritizismus," Letter 10, in *Philosophische Schriften* 1 (Landshut, 1809). See Szondi, *Versuch über das Tragische*, p. 13ff. [This essay on Schelling is included in Szondi, *On Textual Understanding*, chap. 3.]
5. Strindberg, "Der Einakter," p. 341.

9. Constraint and Existentialism

1. Hebbel, foreword to *Maria Magdalena*, in *Sämtliche Werke* 12, ed. R. M. Werner (Berlin, 1904).
2. [Lorca, *The House of Bernarda Alba. A Drama about Women in the Villages of Spain*, in *Three Tragedies*, trans. J. Graham-Lujan and R. O'Connell (New York, 1947), p. 164.]
3. [Ibid., p. 181.]
4. R[udolph] Kassner, "Hebbel," in *Motive* (Berlin, n.d.), p. 185. Also in *Essays* (Leipzig, 1923).
5. Kassner, *Motive*, p. 186.
6. G[unther] Anders, *Kafka, Pro und Kontra* (Munich, 1951) [*Franz Kafka*, trans. A. Steer and A. Torlik (London, 1960)].
7. Sartre, *Huis clos*, in *Théâtre* (Paris, 1947), p. 167 [*No Exit*, in *No Exit and Three other Plays* (New York, 1955), p. 47].
8. Hofmannsthal, *Der Tor und der Tod*, in *Gedichte und lyrische Dramen*, ed. H. Steiner (Stockholm, 1946), p. [202].

IV. Tentative Solutions

10. I Dramaturgy: Expressionism

1. Th[eodor] W. Adorno, *Minima Moralia* (Frankfurt, 1951), p. 197 [*Minima Moralia*, trans. E. F. Jephcott (London, 1974), pp. 149–50].
2. Ibid., p. 203 [p. 154].
3. See the lines cited on pp. 26–27.
4. See p. 27.
5. K[asimir] Edschmid, *Über den Expressionismus in der Literatur und die neue Dichtung* (Berlin, 1919), p. 57.

11. The Political Revue: Piscator

1. E[rwin] Piscator, *Das politische Theater* (Berlin, 1929), p. 128 [*The Political Theater*, trans. H. Rorrison (New York, 1978), p. 185].
2. Ibid., p. 30 [p. 33].
3. Ibid., p. 81f. [pp. 119–20].
4. See pp. 35–36.
5. Piscator, p. 65 [pp. 93–94].
6. Ibid., p. 131f. [p. 187].
7. Ibid., p. 133 [p. 188].

8. Ibid., p. 65 [p. 94].
9. Ibid., p. 150f. [p. 211 f.].
10. Ibid., p. 174 [p. 239], and illustration after p. 176 [p. 200].
11. Ibid., illustration after p. 128 [p. 164].

12. Epic Theater: Brecht

1. Brecht, "Kleines Organon für das Theater," in *Sinn und Form, Sonderheft Bert Brecht* (Potsdam, 1949), p. 17 [in *Brecht on Theatre*, trans. John Willet (New York, 1964), p. 184].
2. Brecht, "Anmerkungen zur Oper Aufsteig und Fall der Stadt Mahagonny" in *Gesammelte Werke* 1 (London, 1938), p. 17 [My translation. For a slightly different version, see Willet, *Brecht on Theatre*, p. 37].
3. Hegel, *Vorlesungen über die Asthetik*, p. 153f. [*Aesthetics*, p. 1158].
4. Brecht, *Die Mutter*, in *Versuche* 7 (Berlin, 1933), p. 4 [*The Mother*, trans. Lee Baxendall (New York, 1965), p. 38].
5. Brecht, "Kleines Organon," p. 28 [Willet, p. 193].
6. Brecht, ["Anmerkungen,"] *Gesammelte Werke* 1, p. 153.
7. "Anmerkungen zu *Die Mutter*," *Die Mutter*, p. 65 [*The Mother*, p. 133].
8. Brecht, "Kleines Organon," p. 36 [Willet, p. 201].
9. Ibid., p. 38 [Ibid., p. 202].

13. Montage: Bruckner

1. See p. 30f.
2. [Ferdinand] Bruckner [pseud. for Theodor Tagger], *Die Verbrecher* (Berlin, 1929).
3. Ibid., p. 77.
4. Ibid., p. 82.
5. Ibid., p. 85.
6. Ibid., p. 99.
7. Ibid., p. 99.
8. Ibid., p. 100.
9. Ibid., pp. 102, 103, 104.
10. See pp. 46–47.
11. See T[heodor] W. Adorno, "Standort des Erzahlers im zeitgenossischen Roman," in [*Noten zur Literatur, Gesammelte Schriften* 2 (Frankfurt, 1974), p. 41f].

14. Enacting the Impossibility of the Drama; Pirandello

1. Pirandello, *Sei personaggi in cerca d'autore*, 3d ed. (Firenze, [1924]), p. 16 [my italics] [*Six Characters in Search of an Author*, trans. E. Storer, in *Naked Masks, Five Plays by Luigi Pirandello*, ed. Eric Bentley (New York, 1952), p. 218].
2. Ibid., p. 34 [p. 226].
3. See pp. 17–18.
4. [*Six Characters*, p. 220].
5. [Ibid., p. 239.]
6. [Ibid., p. 233.]
7. [Ibid., p. 275.]
8. [Ibid., p. 263.]
9. [Ibid., pp. 257–58. See also pp. 242, 256.]
10. [Ibid., p. 258f.]
11. [Ibid., p. 224.]
12. [Ibid., pp. 231–32.]

13. See pp. 30–31 and 35ff.
14. Cf. p. 8f.

15. Monologue Intérieur: *O'Neill*

1. See p. 20f.
2. [Phèdre], Act II, scene 5.
3. [Mary Stuart], Act III, scene 4.
4. Act II, scene 5.
5. See p. 59.
6. Hebbel, *Sämtliche Werke* 2, p. 200f. [*Harod and Miriamne*, trans. Paul Curtis (Chapel Hill, 1950), p. 11].
7. *Sämtliche Werke*, p. 218f. [p. 21].

16. The Epic I as Stage Manager: Wilder

1. See pp. 37–38.
2. See p. 8f.
3. Wilder, *Our Town* (New York, 1938) [p. 64]. [The citations in this translation are from the Avon edition (New York, 1975).]
4. Ibid., p. 97.
5. See "Ibsen," p. 16f.
6. See "Hauptmann," p. 35f.
7. See p. 30f.
8. See p. 36f.
9. See pp. 83–84.
10. See p. 62.
11. *Our Town*, p. 123.
12. Ibid., p. 126.
13. Wilder, "Correspondence with Sol Lesser," in *Theatre Arts Anthology*, ed. R. Gilder (New York, 1950) [pp. 372–73].

17. The Play of Time: Wilder

1. See p. 13f.
2. See p. 9.
3. See Schiller's letter to Goethe of June 18, 1799.
4. See Lukács, *Theorie des Romans*, pp. 12–13 [*Theory of the Novel*, pp. 120–31].
5. Ibid., p. 12 [p. 122].
6. Wilder, *The Long Christmas Dinner* (New York, 1931) [p. 8]. [All citations in this translation are from the Harper edition, *The Long Christmas Dinner and Other Plays in One Act* (New York, 1963).]
7. Ibid., p. 13.
8. Ibid., p. 14.
9. Ibid., p. 18.
10. Ibid., pp. 19–20.
11. Ibid., p. 21.
12. Ibid., p. 23.
13. Ibid., p. 24.
14. Ibid., p. 25.
15. Ibid., p. 17.
16. Ibid., pp. 3, 7, 10, 21.

17. Ibid., pp. 5–6, 7, 13.
18. Ibid., p. 1.

18. Memory: Miller

1. See p. 16.
2. See pp. 47–48.
3. Act II, scene 2.
4. Miller, *Death of a Salesman* (London, 1952) [pp. 44–45]. [All citations in this translation are from the Viking edition (New York, 1958).]
5. Ibid., p. 46.
6. See p. 21f.
7. See p. 17.
8. *Death of a Salesman*, p. 139. [Closing lines not cited.]

Textual Variants

Textual Variants

There are three editions of *Theorie des modernen Dramas*. The first (*E1*) was published in 1956, the second (*E2*) in 1963, both by Suhrkamp Verlag. The second edition includes revisions made by Szondi. The third edition (*E3*), edited by Jean Bollack and others and found in Peter Szondi, *Schriften* 1 (Frankfurt am Main, 1978), was published after Szondi's death and is almost identical to the second edition. Therefore, unless otherwise noted, the variants listed are those found in the first edition when compared to the second revised edition upon which this translation is based.

P. 5.xxv. " . . . existential demands in the Kierkegaardian sense."

P. 11.iv. " . . . the modern play arose must begin by tracing back from the works . . ."

P. 11.vi. " . . . the establishment of such relations" rather than "this kind of back reference."

P. 11.xii. " . . . at first—or occasionally still are . . ."

P. 12.xxiv. "Were . . . one aware . . ."

P. 14.xxv. " . . . in detention . . ."

P. 17.xiv. " . . . namely Captain Alving's . . ."

P. 17.xvi. " . . . that is, Mrs. Alving's . . ."

P. 17.xxxvi. *E1* has no note here. The reference to Szondi's *Versuch uber das Tragische* was added, as indicated in note 2, in "Ibsen."

P. 19.xxxvii. " . . . temporal and psychic absence . . ."

P. 19.xl. "so" does not appear before "the formal."

P. 20.xl. " . . . the loneliness . . ."

P. 27.xvi. "collapse" rather than "cease to be valid."

P. 31.xxviii. "What is simply unbelievable . . . is that . . ."

P. 36.vi, xii. New paragraphs begin with "The dubiousness" and "An action."

P. 36.xxxii. "But, the transformation . . ."

P. 38.xvi. A new paragraph begins with *Before Sunrise.*"

P. 47.xxxi. A new paragraph begins with "In addition."

P. 48.xl. This paragraph begins with "The presentation of another example."

P. 49.vii. "movements" rather than "trends."

P. 49.xl. *E1* adds the following lines: "An adequate discussion of Hofmanns-thal, who (in *Death and the Fool, Yesterday,* and *Zobeida's Wedding*) in large part shares the same thematic as Ibsen, Strindberg, and Chekhov, would require an expansion of this investigation into the field of stylistic criticism. For the same reason, in the pages that follow there will be no examination of the work of T. S. Eliot, whose *Family Reunion* extends Ibsen's analytical technique into the realm of the lyrical. Nor will there be an examination of other authors, such as Giraudoux." The notes that accompany these lines refer the reader to R. Peacock, *The Poet in the Theatre* (London, 1946), concerning Eliot, and to Szondi's "Zu Jean Giraudoux' Amphitryon 380," which was forthcoming at the time in *Neophilologus* 41 (1957), 180–84.

P. 58.xxvi. This comment on the play's actual title is not found in *E1.*

P. 59.xxv. A new paragraph begins with "The dramatist's."

P. 59.xxxi. " . . . the Drama of social convention (Lorca)."

P. 64.xxxiv. In *E1* this comment on German expressionism continues as follows: " . . . group), while the subjective lyric it produced, in which an attempt was made to overcome the feeling of one's own emptiness through a scream, was justifiably forgotten. (And the great exception really is not one, since in Trakel's poems pictures became words.)"

P. 65.xxiv. A new paragraph begins with "The inevitable."

P. 67.xvi. A new paragraph begins with "For Piscator."

P. 71.i. "These changes have the replacement of . . . in common."

P. 73.xxxii. *E3* has no paragraph break at this point.

P. 74.xl. Instead of "proposed," *E1* has "expressed."

P. 85.x. A new paragraph begins with "The representative."

P. 86.xxv. "authorize" rather than "justify."

P. 89.xxx. " . . . to be sure, 'long' . . ."

P. 92.v. Both *E1* and *E2* give Tommy as the son's name; *E3* alone has the correct name, "Larry."

P. 92.xl. A new paragraph begins with "Willy Loman."

P. 93.viii. "Finally, so that his family . . . , Loman commits suicide."

P. 102. note 6. The bibliographical information on Staiger appears only in *E3*, not in the editions published during Szondi's lifetime. *E1* gives p. 8 as the reference, *E2* gives p. 11, *E3* gives p. 12 f. Page 9 seems to be the most likely choice, however.

P. 103. *Ibsen*, note 2. The reference to Szondi's *Versuch über das Tragische* was inserted after that volume was published in 1961. It appears in all but the first edition.

P. 106. *Bruckner*, note 11. In *E1* the reference is to "Form und Gehalt des zeitgenossischen Romans," *Akzente* 1, 1954, p. 410 ff. In *E2* the 1958 edition of *Noten zur Literatur* is cited, but no page reference is given. This translation has therefore used the note appearing in *E3*.

Editor's Notes and Commentary

Editor's Notes and Commentary

P. 3.iv. These lines, which in the German are rendered in a juridical language that would sound strange to the American ear ("Wer aber heute die Entwicklung der neueren Dramatik darzustellen versucht, kann sich zu solchem Richteramt nicht mehr berufen fühlen"), announce two of Szondi's primary concerns: (1) the prior and, for Szondi, erroneous assumption that the function of the critic and criticism is to establish normative judgments about genres and texts, and (2) the failure of critics in the recent past to take responsibility for their method and the results of that method. The historical and ideological as well as critical significance of this insistence on self-conscious criticism is discussed in my foreword to Peter Szondi, *On Textual Understanding*, trans. Harvey Mendelson (Minneapolis, 1986).

P. 3.xx. Szondi introduces the term prehistorical (*vorhistorish*) to point out the difference between theories of the drama that are not conscious of their own historicity and those, like his own, that (drawing on Hegel) examine the historical as well as the aesthetic moments that give rise to new literary or dramatic modes. Nonhistorical theories present their objects as "transhistorical" (*überhistorisch*) entities — ideal theatrical forms that are proposed and examined in terms of "universal" values or norms rather than in terms of their emergence as the formal manifestations of specific socio-historical discourses.

P. 4.v. By citing Hegel in this manner — as a "culminating moment" — Szondi not only introduces one of the "influences" on his own theoretical work (Hegel's notion of a historically based dialectic between form and content) but also points to Hegel's predecessors among the post-Kantian philosophers and writers of the German romantic period. Schelling, Schlegel, Schleiermacher, and Hölderlin are particularly important. See "The Notion of the Tragic in Schelling, Hölderlin, and Hegel," "Friedrich Schlegel's Theory of Poetical Genres," and "Schleiermacher's Hermeneutics Today," in *On Textual Understanding*.

P. 4.xix–xxviii. See Croce, *La poesia* (Bari, 1936), chap. 5. The notion of the three ecstasies of time (*drie Extasen* [*sic*] *der Zeit*) can be found in Staiger's *Grundbegriffe der Poetik*, p. 223. Staiger equates the lyric, epic, and dramatic with the syllable, word, and sentence as embodiments of past, present, and future times. He bases this set of relationships (pp. 203–25) on Heidegger, who discusses past, present, and future as the three ecstasies of temporality (*Ekstasen der Zeitlichkeit*). See *Being and Time*, trans. J. Macquarrie and E. Robinson (New York, 1962), p. 337*n*2.

P 4 xxxvi Adorno applied this chemical metaphor (*niedergeschlagen*) to musical form to clarify the interactive relation between form and content and to propose this relation as the historical basis for the development of all new musical forms. The English translation (*The Philosophy of Modern Music*) loses much of the metaphorical value of the term by translating it as "realization."

P. 4.xli. The thematic (*die Thematik*) is not simply "what the play is about," it is also the conscious or unconscious frame of reference within which the author unfolds the text and the manner in which this set of notions is inscribed in the work. Therefore, as the thematic is materialized in the text, it can cast doubt on formal procedures that, having been elaborated in relation to a different or earlier set of historico-aesthetic expectations, are no longer sufficient to implement this expression. By way of comparison, one can turn to architectural history and note the contradiction between form and thematic that arose when medieval builders tried to construct "gothic" cathedrals with romanesque arches. Szondi's use of "thematic" can be compared to that of the Russian formalists. See, for example, the essay "Thematics," by Boris Tomashevsky, in L. Lemon and M. Rice, eds., *Russian Formalist Criticism* (Lincoln, Nebr., 1965).

P. 5.vii–x. Here Szondi meets head-on the objections of critics who, following Lukács, Hauser, and others, would interpret a text according to a prior and external set of notions about the historical conditions that define the production and meaning of a given work of art. Although from a different point of view, Szondi, like today's "poststructuralist" critics, wants to explore the linguistico-historical context embedded in the text itself rather than to define it through any a priori assumption about social or economic structures.

P. 5.xxxii. This is an echo of Hegel's assertion that "Minerva's owl first takes flight at dusk" — that knowledge of formational processes (for Szondi the interaction between form and content) is possible only when that process is complete. Thus, philosophy and criticism can come into play only at this point as a means of understanding — not of producing — the historical objects from which they abstract their notions. See G. W. F Hegel, *The Philosophy of Right*, trans. T. Knox (London, 1967), p. 13.

P. 6.ii. *Die Dramatik*, the term that Szondi uses here for theatrical works, has no equivalent in English. It means any work written for the stage and also the corpus of plays written at a given time or in a given place. It has been translated as "theatrical works," "dramaturgy," or, simply, "plays," depending on the context.

P. 7.ix. This notion of the "place" at which one acquires being through interaction with others is very similar to that of Heidegger in his discussion of the spatiality of Being (*Dasien*) and its "location" — that is, its grounding in "being-in-the-world," as "being-with," the state of which disclosedness is the constitutive aspect. See *Being and Time*, pp. 149–68.

P. 7.x. In these lines Szondi plays on the possible meanings of *sich entschliesen*, which means "to decide" but also indicates the act of opening up or disclosing one's self: "Der 'Ort' an dem erzu dramatischer Verwirklichung gelangte, war der Akt des Sich-Entschliessens. Indem er sich zur Mitwelt entschloss. . . ."

P. 7.xxii. The plays referred to here are Corneille's *The Cid*, Kleist's *The Broken Jug*, and Hebbel's *Agnes Bernauer*.

P. 8.xiv. Because plays are now to be understood in terms of the dialectical unfolding of particular cultural and aesthetic discourses, all aspects of the Drama and the traditional theories that explain it must be restated within this perspective if they are to be useful in discussing the theatrical event. Thus, Szondi begins a systematic redefinition of the relationship between play and public, of the playing space, and of the normative rules embodied in the three "unities." An entire sociosemiotics of the theater is implicit in this analysis, but it has been only recently that much concrete work has been done in this area. See, for example, the essays in *La relation théâtrale*, ed. Regis Durand (Lille, 1980), and those on the sociology of the theater in *Theater* 15 (Winter, 1983), pp. 5–30.

P. 12.xxiv. Instead of "analytical technique," the term most frequently used in English is "retrospective technique," which renders only part of what Szondi has in mind because it does not convey a sense of the careful exposition and analysis of past events or of the subjective hold these events have on the characters.

P. 12.xxvi. This exchange of letters can be found in J. W. G. Goethe, *Goethe-Schiller Briefe, Gedenkenausgabe der Werke, Briefe und Gespräche* (Zurich, 1949), pp. 334–37, 433–36.

P. 17.xxxix. Szondi keeps the original French in his text: "Nous mourrons tous inconnus."

P. 17.xlii. The "life-lie" is a notion proposed by Dr. Relling, one of the characters in Ibsen's *The Wild Duck*.

P. 18.xii.. Memory and utopia are themes that Szondi examines again in relation to Walter Benjamin. See "Hope in the Past: On Walter Benjamin" in *On Textual Understanding*. In it the terms acquire the added dimension of Benjamin's and Szondi's experience of the effects of the Nazi era on artistic and intellectual life.

P. 24.xl. These lines do not appear in the Swedish original. They were added by Strindberg when he prepared the French version of the play in summer 1887. Szondi was apparently unaware that the German translation he used drew on the French version included here, because he makes no mention of the fact. For further details on the changes Strindberg introduced into this version of his play, see *August Strindbergs Dramer* 3, ed. C. R. Smedmork (Stockholm, 1964), pp. 490–92.

P. 33.xxxiii–xxxix. Szondi cites the French here: "Voila des années et des années que nous sommes ensemble, et nous ne nous sommes jamais aperçus. On dirait que nous sommes toujours seuls! . . . Il faut voir pour aimer."

P. 36.v. "Alienated conditionality" (*entfremdete Zuständlichkeit*), the term Szondi uses here, appears frequently in this volume. It serves to define both the individual isolation and the lack of freedom that distinguishes the characters in the modern drama from their predecessors. Their lives are conditioned by external forces over which they seem to have no control and which deprive them of the will to action that was axiomatic for the characters in earlier drama.

P. 49.xxvii. Szondi cites p. 66 as his reference, but this is obviously an error. The lines can be found on p. 61 of *Grundbegriffe*.

P. 50–51.xxii–i. "Objective spirit" (*objektiver Geist*), a term borrowed from Hegel, is used here as an ironic bit of shorthand. Since, according to Hegel, history is the process of the spirit objectifying itself in the world, those bourgeois dramatists who attempt to "turn back the hands on the clock of the objective spirit" are simply evading the reality of history and the objective cultural developments inherent in it. These dramatists cannot produce what Hegel would call "true" drama, because such drama is always a union of objectivity and subjectivity, of form and content, that is itself a manifestation of the movement of history. See, for example, *Phenomenology of Spirit*, trans. A. Miller (Oxford, 1977), pp. 294–312, and *Aesthetics* 2, trans. T. Knox (Oxford, 1974), pp. 710–13, 1158.

P. 54.viii. *The Difficult Man* was written during and after World War I. Szondi gives the date of its completion, not the date usually provided (1921), which is the date of its first performance.

P. 54.xxiii. Szondi cites the French here: "Misère de l'homme sans Dieu."

P. 54.xxxix. This reference to Staiger is drawn from *Grundbegriffe*, pp. 172–73. Staiger in turn borrowed the notion from Heidegger. The self is in tension—is "ahead of itself"—when it senses its condition of being thrown into existence, of not being complete and closed on itself. See Heidegger, *Being and Time*, pp. 174, 284–85, 321.

P. 56.xl. "Pro-ject" (*Vor-wurf*) is also a term drawn from Staiger. Unfortunately, the double meaning found in the German cannot be duplicated in English. This "pro-ject" is both a casting forward (into life) and the reproach or blame that accompanies the throw as its very condition of being. It is the source of tension in the one-act insofar as it embodies both the causal condition and the trajectory that must be followed so that the play can close on itself and produce meaning or being. See *Grundbegriffe*, pp. 168–75. Cf. Heidegger, *Being and Time*, pp. 174, 219–24.

P. 58.xv. The manner in which Szondi plays with closure, disclosure, and decision here cannot be reproduced in English: "Aber 'Geschlossenheit' und Unfähigkeit zu aller (zwischenmenschlichen) 'Dialektik' zerstorte die Möglichkeit des Dramas, das aus den entschlussen zueinander entschlossener Individuen lebte. . . . "

P. 61.xv. The notion of the *existentialia* appears in *Being and Time*, pp. 70, 79–84. The existential "throw" into existence is discussed in the same work. See my comments regarding the use of "Vor-wurf," by Steiger and Heidegger.

P. 61.xxxviii, xl. In French in Szondi's text: "salon style second empire" and "l'enfer, c'est les autres."

P. 62.xvi, xxii. Szondi uses the French title, *Huis Clos*.

P. 67.xv. The paragraphing in Szondi's text is not the same as that in Piscator's. It is the latter that appears in this translation.

P. 76.xl. Although Szondi does not develop this idea, it marks an important point in his overall argument: in the modern era, even if it is possible to give form to the alienation of the past from the present, the subject from the object, the "logocentric" desire to overcome or dissimulate this difference remains strong. Here Szondi links this desire to mass culture. On this subject see Max Horkheimer and T. W. Adorno, *Dialectics of Enlightenment*, trans. J. Cumming (New York, 1972); Thomas Crow, "Modernism and Mass Culture," in *Modernism and Modernity*, ed. S. Guilbaut and

D. Sokins (Halifax and New York, 1983); Fredric Jameson, "Reification and Utopia in Mass Culture," in *Social Text* 1, (Winter 1979); and Walter Benjamin, "The Work of Art in the Age of Mechanical Reproducibility," in *Illuminations* (New York, 1969).

P. 77.ii. Szondi uses the Italian title of Pirandello's play throughout this essay: *Si personaggi in cerca d'autore*.

P. 77.xx. Szondi cites these lines in the original Italian: "L'autore che ci creò, vivi, non volle poi, *o non potè* materialmente metterci al mondo dell'arte."

P. 77.xli. Quoted in Italian by Szondi: "Ho sempre avuto di questa maledette aspirazioni a una certa solida sanità morale."

P. 81.xii. To avoid frequent repetition of the German equivalent of "aside," Szondi chose to use *à part*, a term derived from the French. This translation has retained his usage to give a clearer sense of Szondi's prose as well as to avoid the same repetition problem.

P. 84.xv. Szondi discusses the deconstructive tendencies in romantic literature in some detail in "Friedrich Schlegel and Romantic Irony." See *On Textual Understanding*, chap. 4.

P. 88.xviii. A comparison of the notions of desire and memory as they appear in Proust and Benjamin can be found in the previously cited essay "Hope in the Past."

P. 90.ii. Müller discusses "narrative time/narrated time" in *Gestaltung-Umgestaltung in Wilhelm Meisters Lerhjahre* (Halle, 1948), p. 33.

P. 93.xxxi. Szondi's citation from *Hamlet* is in English.

Index

Index

125

Peter Szondi was head of the Institute for General and Comparative Literature at the Free University of West Berlin and then, shortly before his death in 1971, he was appointed to a similar position at the University of Zürich. A collection of his essays, *On Textual Understanding*, was published by Minnesota in 1986.

Michael Hays is associate professor of theater studies at Cornell University. He is author of *The Public and Performance: Essays on the History of French and German Theatre, 1870–1900*; he also served as editor of *The Criticism of Peter Szondi*, a special issue of *boundary 2* (1983).

Jochen Schulte-Sasse is professor of German and comparative literature at the University of Minnesota, and co-editor of the series Theory and History of Literature.